"BEHOLD THEIR PRIDE, AND SEND YOUR WRATH UPON THEIR HEADS; GIVE TO ME, A WIDOW, THE STRENGTH TO DO WHAT I PLAN." - JUDITH 9:9
AF270258

JUDITH
Captive to Conqueror

Written by Gabrielle Gniewek

Illustrated by Sean Lam

Pauline
BOOKS & MEDIA
BOSTON

Library of Congress Control Number: 2024939185

ISBN 10: 0-8198-3176-X
ISBN 13: 978-0-8198-3176-7

Story by Gabrielle Gniewek
Art by Sean Lam

Published by Pauline Books & Media, 50 Saint Paul's Avenue, Boston, MA 02130-3491

Printed in the U.S.A.

JCTC VSAUSAPEOILL7-1510211 3176-X

www.pauline.org

Pauline Books & Media is the publishing house of the Daughters of St. Paul, an international congregation of women religious serving the Church with the communications media.

1 2 3 4 5 6 7 8 9   28 27 26 25 24

WHOOOOOOOSH
WHOOOSH
DRIP DRIP
SPLATTER
AHHHHHGH!

PANT
PANT
THUD
WHEEZE
ROLL
ROLL
E-ECBATANA WILL NEVER FALL!...

ESPECIALLY TO THE LIKES OF YOU!
HMM. NOW, I FIND THAT HARD TO BELIEVE, BECAUSE...

IT ALREADY HAS.
THUD

HEH.
WELL, MY LORD...IT LOOKS LIKE THE MIGHTY MEDES HAVE A NEW KING NOW.
NO. THEY HAVE SHOWN ME NO RESPECT AS A KING...
SHATTER
I AM GOD.

I DON'T SEE HIM...I LOOK EVERYWHERE BUT CAN NEVER SEEM TO FIND HIM.
THAT'S WHEN I REALIZE...

HE NEVER REALLY LEAVES MY SIDE.
JUDITH...
JUDITH...

TIME TO GET UP, MY LADY.
I TOLD YOU NOT TO CALL ME THAT.

SORRY, JUDITH... HERE'S YOUR WASH BOWL.
REMEMBER THAT IT'S MARKET DAY TODAY. I HEARD NATHAN WILL BE SELLING POMEGRANATES AGAIN TODAY.
FWSSSSH...
LOOKS LIKE IT'S GOING TO BE ANOTHER HOT ONE.
DRIBBLE
THE COOK IS MAKING YOUR FAVORITE FOR BREAKFAST...IT SMELLS SO GOOD, SHE ACTUALLY HAD TO CHASE ME OUT OF THE KITCHEN!

WHAT'S WRONG, JUDITH?
DO I TREAT YOU WELL? I MEAN, DO I TELL YOU... HOW MUCH I APPRECIATE YOU?
YOU REALLY MISS HIM DON'T YOU?
HEH.
IT'S BEEN THREE YEARS NOW... YOU'D THINK I'D BE OVER IT.
I DON'T THINK SO.

BECAUSE, IF YOU REALLY LOVE SOMEONE...
THEY NEVER REALLY LEAVE YOU.
COME ON...
LET'S GET SOME BREAKFAST.
DON'T YOU GO ANYWHERE SOON.
WEEEEE

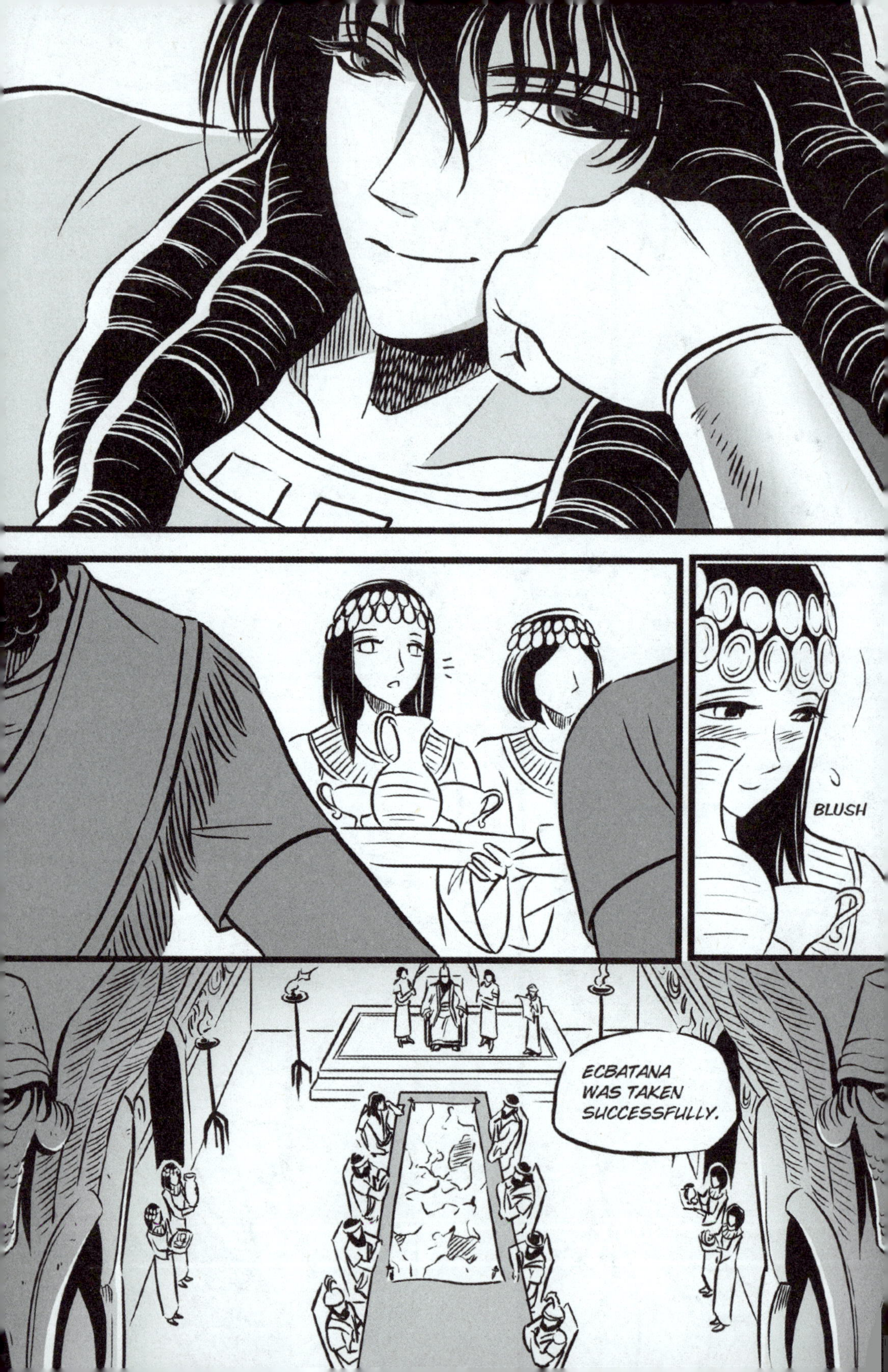
BLUSH
ECBATANA WAS TAKEN SUCCESSFULLY.

2ND IN COMMAND LIEUTENANT ASHUR CONQUERED THE MEDES IN THE BATTLE ON THE PLAINS, AND IS HONORED HERE TONIGHT.
AND ARPHAXAD, THE LATE KING OF THE MEDES, FELL AT THE HANDS OF GENERAL HOLOFERNES...
...WHOM WE ALSO HONOR HERE TONIGHT.
GLARE
HIS MAJESTY HAS ALSO GAINED CONTROL OVER THE CHALDEAN CITIES ALONG THE EUPHRATES, TIGRIS, AND HYDASPES THROUGH OUR ALLIANCE DURING THE WAR...

A NUMBER OF UPRISINGS HAVE OCCURRED ALL OVER ECBATANA, WHEN THE PEOPLE HEARD OF THE LATE KING'S DEATH.
SLAM!
IF THEY DON'T RESPECT ME... I'LL MAKE THEM WORSHIP ME!
ANYONE WHO GOES AGAINST MY WILL... WILL SUFFER MY WRATH.

YOU'VE ALREADY TAKEN THEIR LAND AND WOMEN, AND DRAFTED OR KILLED THEIR MEN—
GLARE
...AS...YOU SHOULD HAVE.
WE COULD DEMOLISH THEIR GOD'S TEMPLE, AND RAISE A NEW ONE TO YOU!
JUST SAY THE WORD AND I'LL LEAD THE BATTALION MYSELF!

WHAT DO YOU THINK, HOLOFERNES?
HMM.
THEN AGAIN...
SOUNDS LIKE A GOOD IDEA...
WHAT?

I'M NOT SURE A SIMPLE TEMPLE WILL BE ENOUGH TO ATONE...BUT...
CHINK
HIS MAJESTY THE GOD-KING HAS BEEN GREATLY DISHONORED.
AND HOW MANY JOINED?
HOW MANY NATIONS WERE ASKED TO JOIN HIS MAJESTY IN THE BATTLE AGAINST ARPHAXAD?
MORE THAN TWENTY.

ONLY THE CHALDEANS...
MY LORD, CAN WE AFFORD TO MAKE THAT MANY ENEMIES? OUR MILITARY—
—IS THE LARGEST IN THE WORLD.
A GOD SHOULD RULE THE WHOLE EARTH SHOULD HE NOT? WHY HAVE ONE TEMPLE WHEN YOU CAN HAVE HUNDREDS?
YES...I'LL MAKE THEM ALL PAY. LORD ASHUR WILL LEAD MY TROOPS AND—

FSHH
AHHHGGH!
STAB

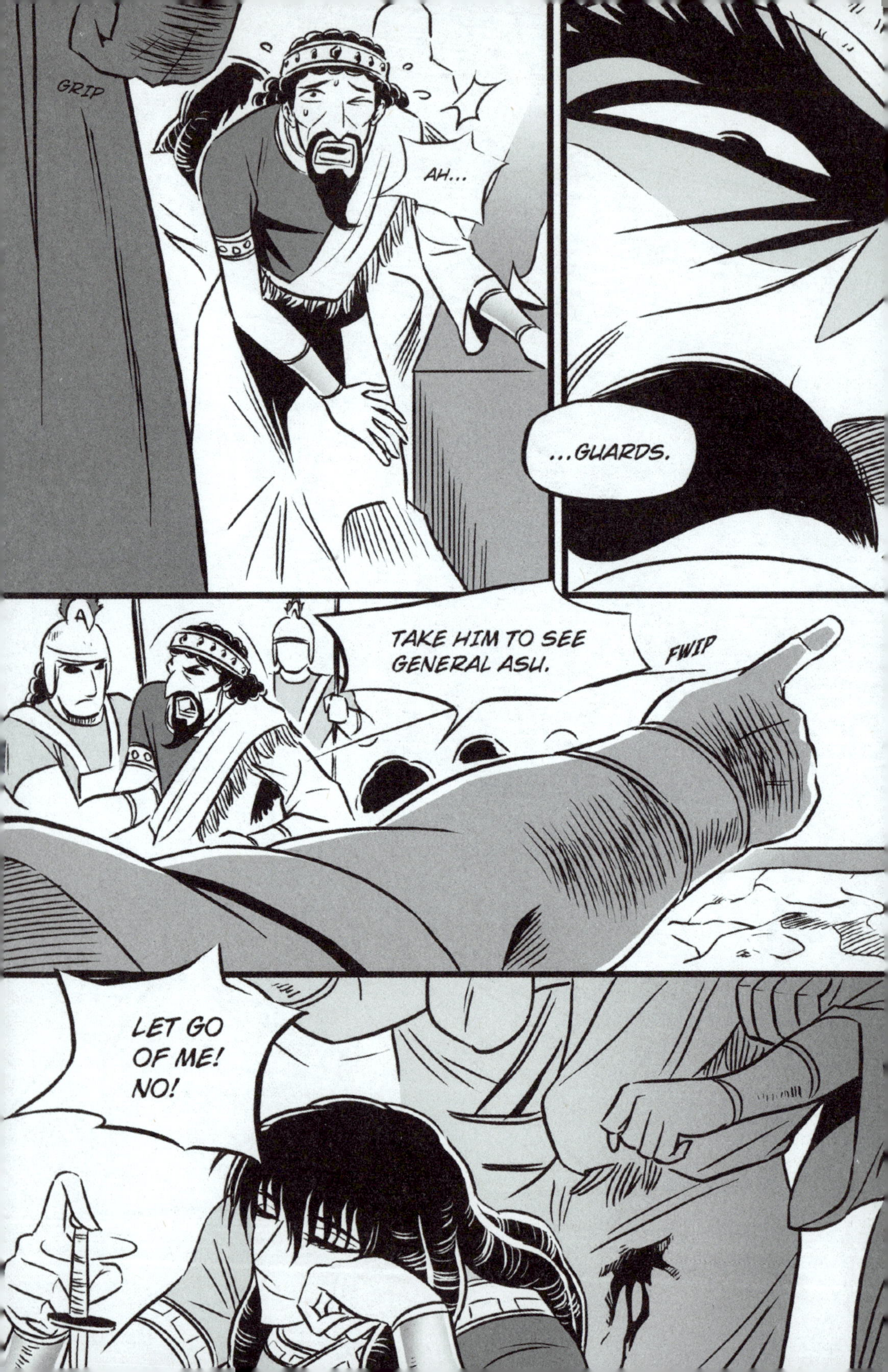

GRIP
AH...
...GUARDS.
TAKE HIM TO SEE GENERAL ASU.
FWIP
LET GO OF ME! NO!

NO! NOOOO!
HOLOFERNES...
YOU ARE NOW LIEUTENANT OF THE ASSYRIAN ARMY, AND 2ND IN COMMAND. YOU WILL GO IN ASHUR'S STEAD.
YES YOUR MAJESTY...

WHY, HELLO, JUDITH!
BUSTLE
BUSTLE
CHATTER!
WHAT CAN I GET YOU TODAY?
I'D LIKE SOME OF THOSE POMEGRANATES.
THAT'LL BE ONE SHEKEL.

YOU'RE FAR TOO MODEST.
AND YOU ALWAYS PAY TOO MUCH.
RUSTLE
YOU HAVE SEVEN CHILDREN.
AND NOW YOU HAVE SEVEN POMEGRANATES.
...ARE YOU SURE?
WELL, IF YOU'RE GOING TO BE THAT GENEROUS...

AT LEAST TAKE THIS LOAF OF BREAD I MADE AS WELL.
WE'RE GOING TO RUN THESE TO SOME NEEDY FAMILIES... BUT WE MADE TOO MANY... PLEASE?
ALRIGHT, JUDITH... IF IT MAKES YOU FEEL BETTER, I'LL TAKE A LOAF OF BREAD.
HERE.

HAVE A NICE DAY!
LOOK!
SPLIT
PAPA!
WHAT IS THAT?

TEN SHEKELS??
JUDITH! I CAN'T-
HEH
SHE'S RESOURCEFUL... I'LL GIVE HER THAT MUCH.

BUSTLE
BUSTLE
BUSTLE
HERE JUDITH, LET ME HAVE THAT.
DON'T EVEN THINK ABOUT IT. I CAN HANDLE A BAG OF FRUIT.
YOINK
NOW THAT I MENTION IT... WHY DON'T YOU LET ME TAKE SOME OF THAT?

OH PLEASE, MY LADY!
... THANK YOU, JUDITH.
GLARE
OH, ZUSA. I HOPE YOU KNOW HOW MUCH YOU MEAN TO ME. I ALWAYS MEAN TO TELL YOU...
BUT I CAN NEVER SEEM TO FIND THE WORDS...

I BROUGHT YOU WATER.
IS THAT ALL YOU CAME OUT FOR?
YOU'LL DEHYDRATE IF YOU DON'T DRINK SOMETHING.
THE SIGHT OF YOU IS MORE REFRESHING THAN ANY WATER YOU COULD BRING.
SLOSH
OH SHUSH, YOU. NOW DRINK YOUR WATER.

RUSTLE
PAT
WHO WOULD'VE THOUGHT I'D MARRY THE MOST BEAUTIFUL WOMAN IN THE WORLD?
MANASSEH! STOP!

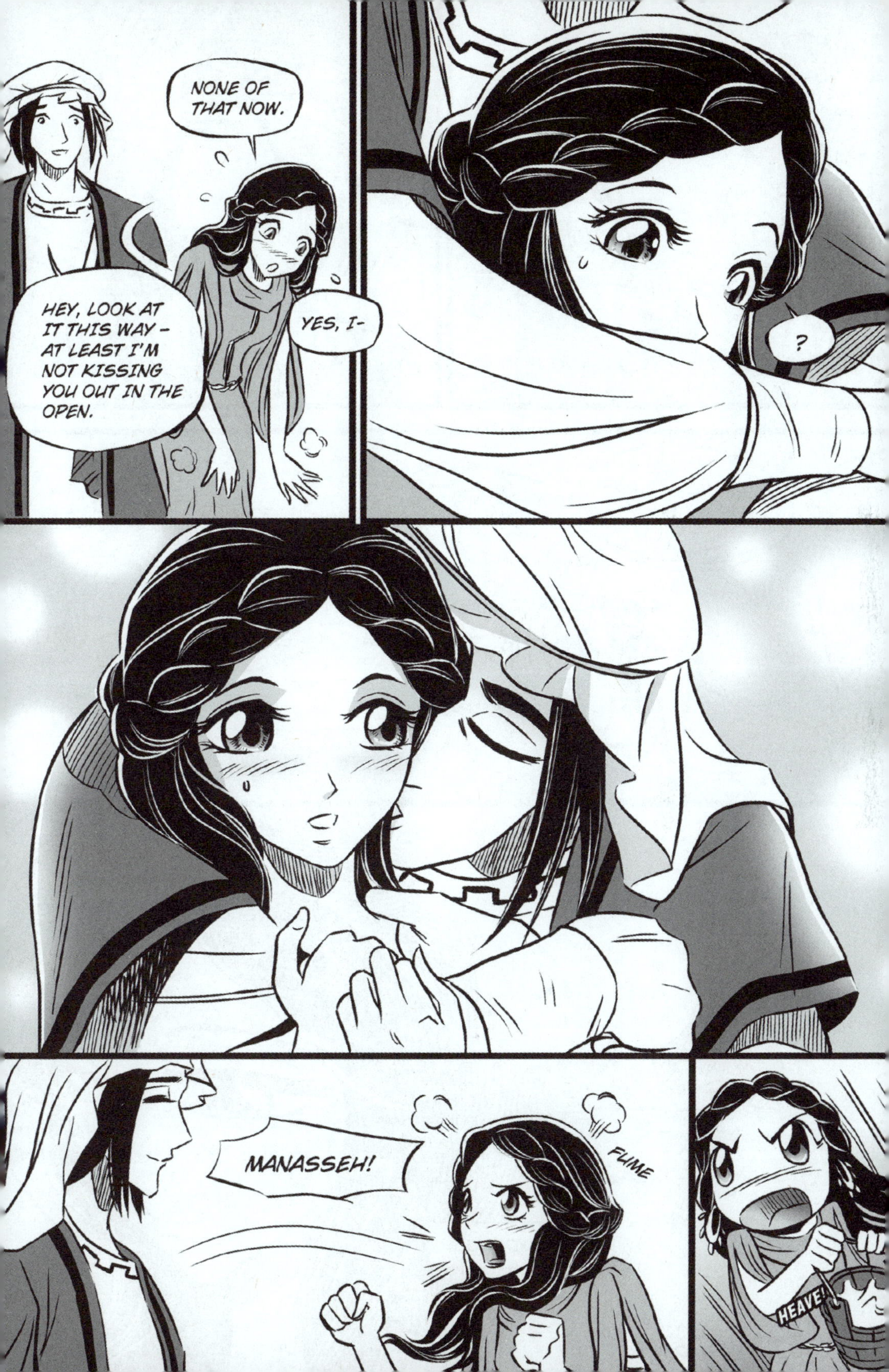

NONE OF THAT NOW.
HEY, LOOK AT IT THIS WAY – AT LEAST I'M NOT KISSING YOU OUT IN THE OPEN.
YES, I-
?
MANASSEH!
FUME
HEAVE

HMPH
I LOVE YOU!
I LOVE YOU TOO.

... AND IF SOMETHING EVER HAPPENED TO YOU, ZUSA, I'D WANT YOU TO KNOW.

WHAT IS IT?

CROUCH
WHAT IS YOUR NAME, CHILD?
EMANUEL... WHAT A STRONG NAME.
EMANUEL.
IF I EVER HAD A SON, I THINK I MIGHT NAME HIM THAT TOO.

TAKE CARE OF THEM, EMANUEL.
LOOK! LOOK!

YOU, HOLOFERNES, WILL HEAD THIS PUNITIVE CAMPAIGN.
FWOOSH
CRACKLE
CRACKLE

KRAASH!
TAKE YOUR FORCES AND STORM THE GATES OF PERSIA, SAMARIA, GOSHEN, EGYPT... TAKE EVERY CITY YOU COME ACROSS.
ANY CITIES THAT DO NOT SURRENDER IMMEDIATELY... ANY COUNTRIES THAT RESIST IN ANY WAY...
CLANG
RAAAAA!
CLASH

TAKE THEM BY FORCE.

KILL THEIR MEN... TAKE THEIR WOMEN...

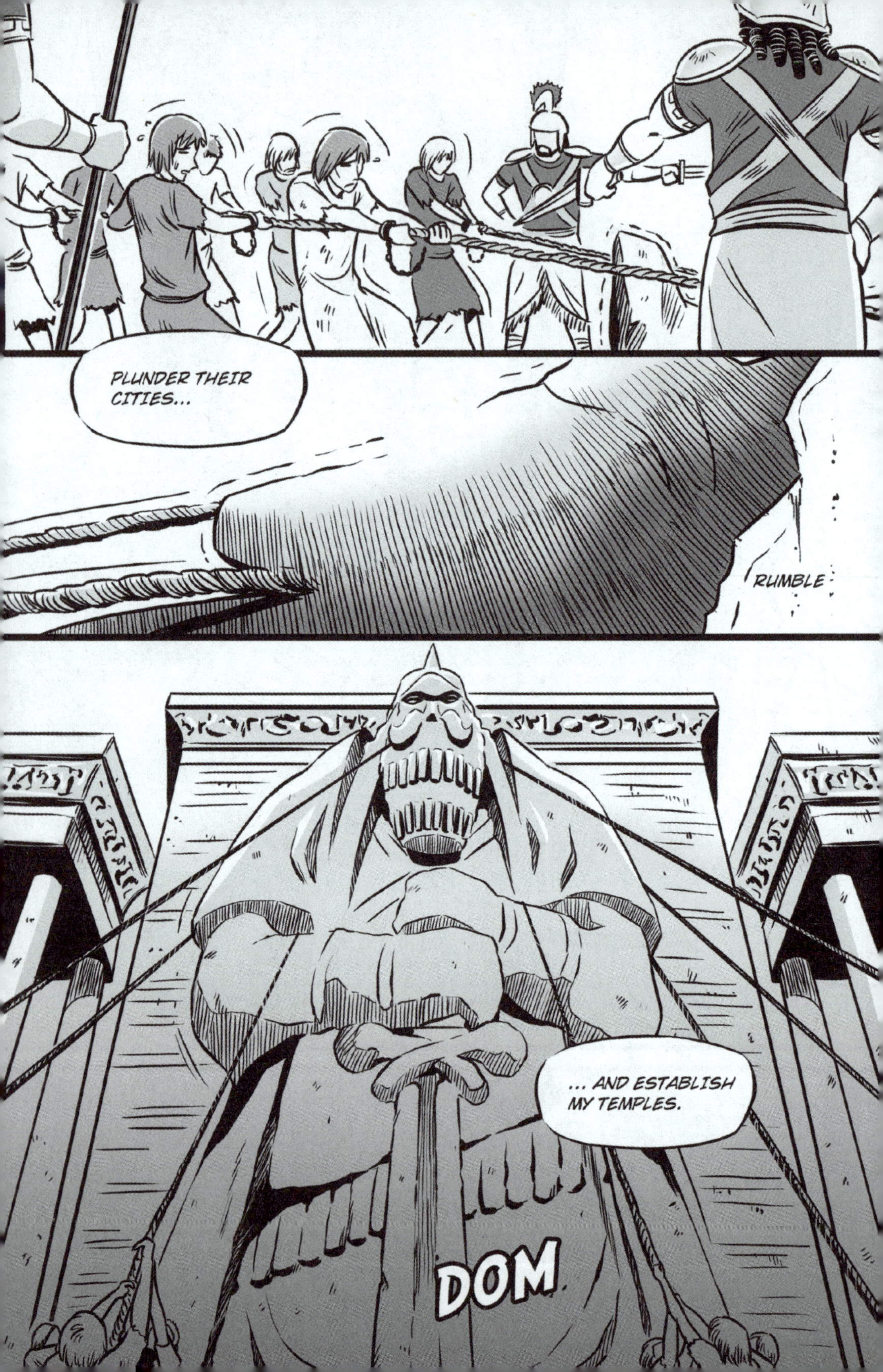
PLUNDER THEIR CITIES...
RUMBLE
... AND ESTABLISH MY TEMPLES.
DOM

SHOW THEM I AM A POWER WORTHY OF FEARFUL WORSHIP.
MILCOM, HELP US.

TAP
TAP
TAP

KOHEN GADOL!
HIGH PRIEST JOAKIM!

CAN SOMEONE PLEASE TELL ME WHERE TO FIND THE HIGH PRIEST!?
WHAT NEWS DO YOU BRING?
WHAT IS IT, MY SON?
HOLOFERNES' ARMY IS HEADED THIS WAY! ALL OF THE OTHER NATIONS HAVE FALLEN! THE ISRAELITES ARE THE ONLY ONES LEFT!

OH GOSH!
MURMUR
MURMUR
CALM DOWN. WE ALL KNEW THIS DAY WOULD COME — IT WAS ONLY A MATTER OF TIME.
HE ORDERS THAT OUR BORDERING CITIES OPEN THEIR GATES AND SURRENDER!
ANY ACTION OTHERWISE WILL BE CONSIDERED AN ACT OF RETALIATION, AND WE WILL BE TAKEN BY FORCE!... THE CITIES AWAIT YOUR ORDERS!
HOW FAR AWAY IS HE?
STROKE

FROM THE BORDER? ONE DAY? MAYBE TWO?
THEN THERE'S NOT A MOMENT TO LOSE!
SEND WORD TO ALL OF THE BORDERING CITIES TO ESTABLISH FORTRESSES, STOCKPILE PROVISIONS, AND AWAIT INSTRUCTIONS FOR STATIONING THE MEN IN STRATEGIC POSITIONS!
NOD
NOD
GO THROUGHOUT ISRAEL AND TELL THE PEOPLE TO PRAY AND DO PENANCE...BY GOD'S WILL WE WILL NOT GO INTO CAPTIVITY WHEN WE'VE JUST RETURNED FROM IT.

AND YOU! RIDE HARD, RIDE FAST, AND GET TO BETHULIA BEFORE HOLOFERNES DOES. TELL THEM DO NOT SURRENDER. TELL THEM REINFORCEMENTS ARE ON THEIR WAY.
TAP
TAP
WHY BETHULIA, JOAKIM?
IF WHAT WE HAVE HEARD LAST OF HOLOFERNES' MOVEMENTS IS TRUE, THEN HE'LL BE COMING FROM THE SOUTHWEST. BETHULIA WILL BE STRUCK FIRST.

THEY ARE THE ONLY MAJOR OUTPOST IN THAT DIRECTION.
BETHULIA IS OUR ONLY DEFENSE SEPARATING THE CAPITAL FROM HOLOFERNES.
COME... LET US PRAY.

AM I GOING TO DIE?
SHUFFLE
SHUFFLE
WHERE ELSE WOULD THEY BE TAKING ALL OF THE CONQUERED KINGS?
WELL, THEY SAY YOUR LIFE IS SUPPOSED TO FLASH BEFORE YOUR EYES PRIOR TO DYING — AND THAT HASN'T HAPPENED YET.

SO IT EITHER MEANS I'M NOT DYING... THE RUMOR'S A LIE... OR I HAVEN'T LIVED THAT MUCH OF A LIFE...PROBABLY THE LATTER.
I DON'T KNOW, I TRIED TO DO WHAT WAS BEST FOR MY PEOPLE. SURRENDERING SOUNDED LIKE THE RIGHT IDEA AT THE TIME... I MEAN, IT'S ONLY A TEMPLE RIGHT?
BUT LEAVING THE PEOPLE IN HIS HANDS... NOW I'M NOT SO SURE.

WELL, THIS COULD BE IT. BETTER GO OUT SMILING.
SHUFFLE
SHUFFLE
THEY HAVE ARRIVED, MY LORD.
MY LORDS! PLEASE! COME IN. MAKE YOURSELVES COMFORTABLE.

...CREAK
IS THAT HIM?
IS THAT HOLOFERNES?

PLEASE, MY LORDS, THERE IS NOTHING TO FEAR. PUT YOUR- SELVES AT EASE.
WELL IT'S BETTER THAN EXECUTION.
FWUMP

THANK YOU, EVERYONE. I CALLED YOU ALL HERE TODAY FOR ONE PURPOSE...
EACH AND EVERY ONE OF YOU IS HURT, CONFUSED, AND WARY...
ANGRY AND SCARED... I CAN SEE THAT.
YOUR UNMERITED SUFFERINGS HAVE MOVED ME, DEEPLY... MY LORDS, I HAVE SUMMONED YOU ALL TOGETHER SO THAT...
I CAN FEEL YOUR SADNESS OVER YOUR LOSSES, AND WHAT A WEIGHT IT IS TO CARRY...

TIP
... I MIGHT APOLOGIZE, AND PERHAPS ATONE FOR WHAT KING NEBUCHADNEZZAR HAS ORDERED DONE TO YOU.
BOW
BUT YOU'RE THE ONE THAT BURNED OUR CITIES AND RAZED OUR TEMPLES!
WHAT?
I DON'T UNDERSTAND...
YES, AND IT WAS TRULY WRONG OF ME TO DO SO... BUT CAN YOU BLAME ME?

EACH AND EVERY ONE OF YOU NOBLE MEN WOULD BE WILLING TO SACRIFICE ANYTHING TO PROTECT YOUR PEOPLE WITHOUT HESITATION, WOULDN'T YOU?
WHAT DO YOU MEAN?
OF COURSE!
I TOO WAS A KING LIKE ALL OF YOU... AND NEBUCHADNEZZAR THREATENED TO SLAUGHTER ALL MY PEOPLE IF I DID NOT BEND TO HIS WILL.

I DID NOT WANT TO BRING HARM TO OTHERS... I ONLY SOUGHT TO PROTECT MY PEOPLE.

EVERY CRIME, EVERY WRONG I COMMITTED... I DID TO SAVE THOSE IN MY CARE.

AND I ASK YOU, FELLOW FATHERS OF NATIONS... IF ANY OF YOU WOULDN'T DO THE SAME TO PROTECT THE ONES YOU LOVE?

WOULDN'T YOU DO ABSO-LUTELY ANYTHING TO KEEP THEM FROM HARM?

REGARDLESS -- I OWE YOU ALL MY HUMBLEST APOLOGIES, NOT ONLY FOR WHAT I WAS FORCED TO DO... BUT FOR ALL THE EVILS, AND WRONGS NEBUCHADNEZZAR HAS DONE TO YOU.
I KNOW I'D DO ANYTHING...
YEAH! THE REAL PROBLEM IS NEBUCHADNEZZAR!
AFTER ALL, HE'S THE ONE THAT'S REALLY BEHIND ALL THIS!
PLEASE UNDERSTAND, I CANNOT RETURN YOU ALL TO YOUR THRONES, FOR IF NEBUCHADNEZZAR FOUND OUT, MY PEOPLE WOULD BE SLAUGHTERED!

THE MOST I CAN DO TO ATONE FOR MY SINS...
IS GRANT YOU ALL YOUR FREEDOM!
THE WICKED NEBUCHADNEZZAR ORDERED YOU ALL KILLED, BUT I CANNOT. NO. I WILL NOT BRING MYSELF TO FOLLOW THROUGH WITH SUCH A HEINOUS COMMAND.
AFTER ALL HE'S DONE TO YOU, USING ME AS HIS PUPPET. I WANT TO GIVE YOU ALL A FIGHTING CHANCE TO START ANEW. I KNOW IT ISN'T MUCH, BUT PLEASE...

DON
... ACCEPT MY HUMBLE OFFERING.
AND I HOPE THAT YOU CAN FIND IT IN YOUR HEARTS TO FORGIVE A WRETCH LIKE ME FOR ALL I'VE DONE.

PLEASE, MY LORD!
PLEASE RISE!
DON'T TAKE THE BLAME FOR HIM! YOU'RE JUST ANOTHER INNOCENT VICTIM LIKE US!
MY LORD, FOR SOMEONE WHO HAS SUFFERED AS MUCH AS WE HAVE, YOU ARE TOO HARD ON YOURSELF.
YOU ARE TOO KIND TO THIS COWARD, GOOD SIRS. AND WHAT I GIVE YOU IS NOT NEARLY ENOUGH...
YOU HAVE GIVEN US OUR LIVES BACK.

BUT WHERE WILL YOU ALL GO? WHAT IF I AM SENDING YOU ALL DOWN THE PATH OF A DRIFTER? A PATH THAT LEADS ONLY TO POVERTY AND STARVATION?
YOU HAVE GIVEN US A SECOND CHANCE WHEN DEATH WAS OUR ONLY FUTURE... HOW COULD WE ASK FOR MORE?
IT SIMPLY WILL NOT SUFFICE! I AM DETERMINED TO UNDO WHAT NEBUCHADNEZZAR HAS DONE TO THE BEST OF MY ABILITY... I KNOW!...
WHY DON'T I EMPLOY YOU ALL??
SHFFT

EMPLOY?

YES! YOU ARE ALL MEN OF LEADERSHIP, AND EXPERTS OF MILITARY UNDERSTANDING!... YOUR COUNSEL WOULD BE MOST APPRECIATED IN MY COURT!

YOU HAVE GIVEN OUR LIVES PURPOSE AGAIN, LORD HOLOFERNES! NOW WE ARE INDEBTED TO YOU. WE WILL SERVE YOU IN ALL YOU COMMAND.

CLAP

CLAP

CLAP

CLAP
CLAP
CLAP
CLAP
CLAP
CLAP
THANK YOU ALL!
WHY DON'T WE TAKE A SHORT BREAK, AND RESUME IN A HALF-HOUR'S TIME? HMM?
MY LORD, ARE YOU SURE THIS IS WISE?

HEE HEE!
GIGGLE
GIGGLE
GURGLE
GURGLE
WELCOME BACK LORD HOLOFERNES!
FOOMP
WE MISSED YOU!
NOT AS MUCH AS I MISSED YOU...

ARE YOU SURE THIS IS A GOOD IDEA SIR?
WHAT IF NEBUCHADNEZZAR —

YES, BAGOAS, I'M VERY AWARE OF THE RISK.

WOULDN'T IT BE EASIER JUST TO KILL THEM, MY LORD?

PROBABLY.
TWIRL
HERE.
BUT WE SAW HOW MUCH GOOD THAT DID IN MAKING THE PEOPLE OF ECBATANA SUBMISSIVE.
AND BESIDES...
YOU SHOULD ALWAYS KEEP YOUR FRIENDS CLOSE... AND YOUR ENEMIES CLOSER. LONG ENOUGH TO GET WHAT YOU NEED FROM THEM ANYWAY...

NOW, I NEED ALL OF YOUR EXPERTISE...
NEBUCHADNEZZAR HAS ORDERED ME TO TAKE THE NATION OF ISRAEL NEXT.
WHAT DO YOU PLAN TO DO?

THERE'S NO WAY AROUND IT... WE CAN'T FOOL NEBUCHADNEZZAR ON A SCALE AS LARGE AS THE CAPTURE OF AN ENTIRE CITY.
SIGH
I HATE TO SAY IT, BUT THE ONLY WAY TO SAVE THEM, US, AND OUR PEOPLE, IS TO TAKE THEIR CITY...
ARE YOU SURE?
I SHUDDER TO THINK WHAT HORRORS HE WILL DO IF WE DON'T FOLLOW HIS ORDERS... DO YOU ALL UNDERSTAND THE SITUATION?
NOD
NOD
WHAT ABOUT THE PEOPLE OF ISRAEL? WON'T WE BE HURTING THEM?

I KNOW ALL OF YOU ARE EXPERTS, AND HAVE DEALT WITH THEM IN THE PAST... IT'S THE ONLY WAY WE CAN ALL SURVIVE.
WHICH IS WHY I NEED ALL OF YOUR KNOWLEDGE OF THE ISRAELITES IN ORDER TO MAKE THIS DEFEAT AS QUICK AS POSSIBLE WITH THE LEAST AMOUNT OF CASUALTIES.
GLARE
WELL, THEIR CAPITAL IS JERUSALEM, HERE.
YES, I SEE... AND WHAT ARE THESE MOUNTAINS HERE?

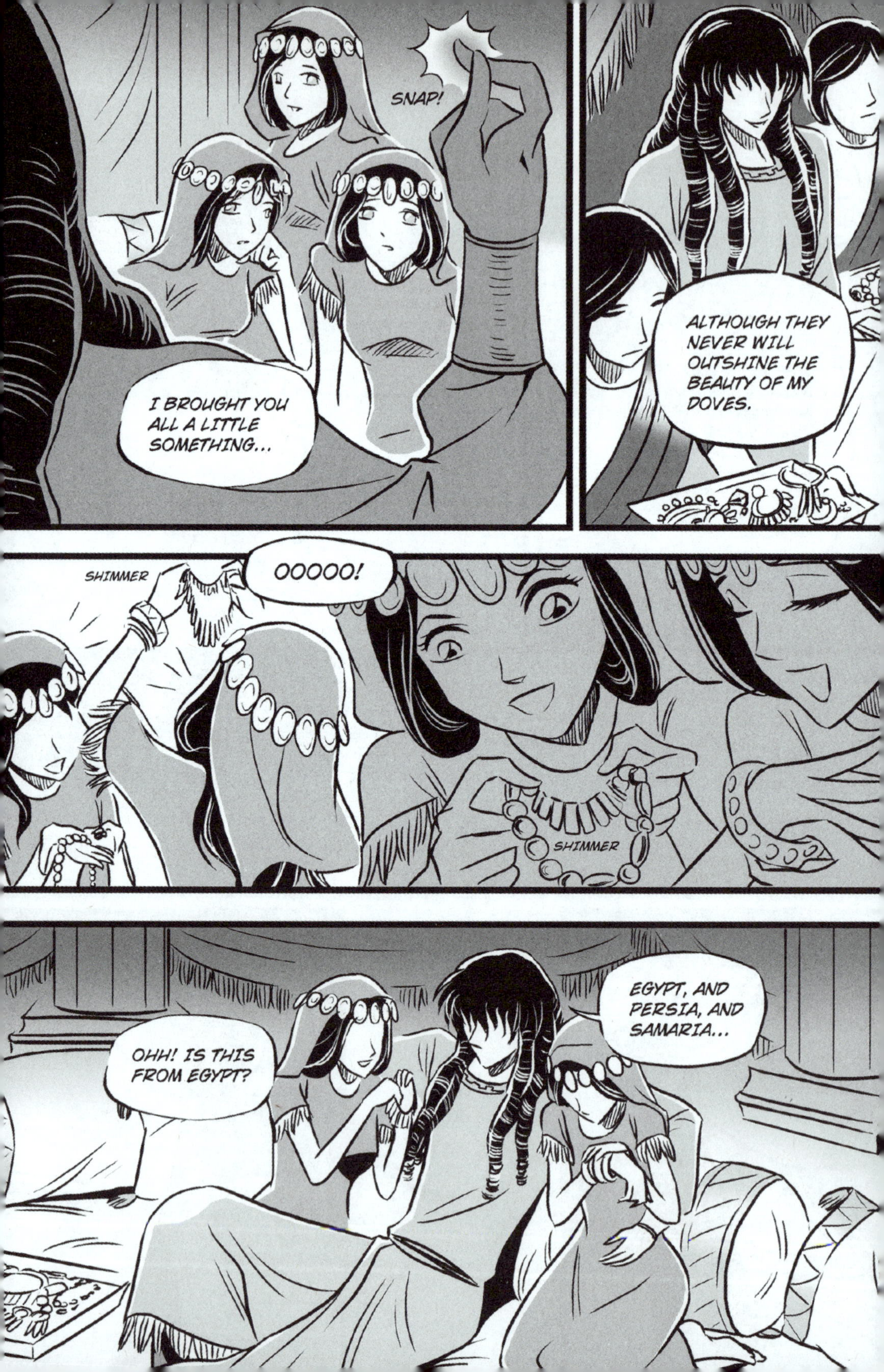

SNAP!
I BROUGHT YOU ALL A LITTLE SOMETHING...
ALTHOUGH THEY NEVER WILL OUTSHINE THE BEAUTY OF MY DOVES.
SHIMMER
OOOOO!
SHIMMER
OHH! IS THIS FROM EGYPT?
EGYPT, AND PERSIA, AND SAMARIA...

THEY'RE BEAUTIFUL MY LORD!

BEAUTIFUL GIRLS SHOULD HAVE BEAUTIFUL THINGS... I HOPE YOU ENJOY THEM.

OH YES, MY LORD.

BUT NOT NEARLY AS MUCH AS WE ENJOY YOUR COMPANY.

PLEASE DON'T LEAVE US AGAIN FOR ANOTHER BORING MEETING.

I DON'T KNOW LADIES, I'M PRETTY BORED HERE TOO...

YOU MIGHT HAVE TO ENTERTAIN ME.

YOUR MAJESTY...
GIGGLE
LORD ACHIOR REQUESTS AN AUDIENCE WITH YOU.

... I AM SORRY MY DOVES.
SIGH

SEND HIM IN, BAGOAS.
DON'T TAKE TOO LONG.

RUSTLE

UH...
THANKS.

WELCOME,
ACHIOR.
WHAT CAN I
DO FOR YOU?

HEY, YOUR MAJESTY,
OR, MY LORD... I JUST
CAME TO SAY, WELL,
IT'S PROBABLY A BAD
IDEA TO GO TO WAR
AGAINST ISRAEL.

HMM?...
WHY'S THAT?

SPIN

WELL, TO PUT IT SIMPLY—
PLEASE DO.
...THE ISRAELITES ARE UNDEFEATABLE.
THEY WORSHIP THIS GOD THAT DELIVERS THEM FROM ALL THEIR FOES SO LONG AS THEY FOLLOW HIS ORDINANCES...
BUT THE MOMENT THEY SINNED AGAINST HIM, THEY WENT RIGHT BACK INTO CAPTIVITY.
I'M NOT SAYING I BELIEVE IN THEIR GOD OR ANYTHING... OR ANY GOD FOR THAT MATTER...

BUT IF THEY HAVEN'T DISOBEYED THEIR GOD'S LAWS RECENTLY, WE SHOULDN'T RISK IT.
TINK
IF YOU DON'T BELIEVE IN SUPERSTITIONS, THEN WHY DO YOU WORRY?
IF THE RUMOR'S FALSE, THEN THERE'S NO REASON TO WORRY... BUT IF IT'S TRUE, MY SOLDIERS ARE NOW STATIONED IN YOUR RANKS, AND I—
YOUR SOLDIERS ARE NO LONGER YOUR CONCERN.
WHAT?...

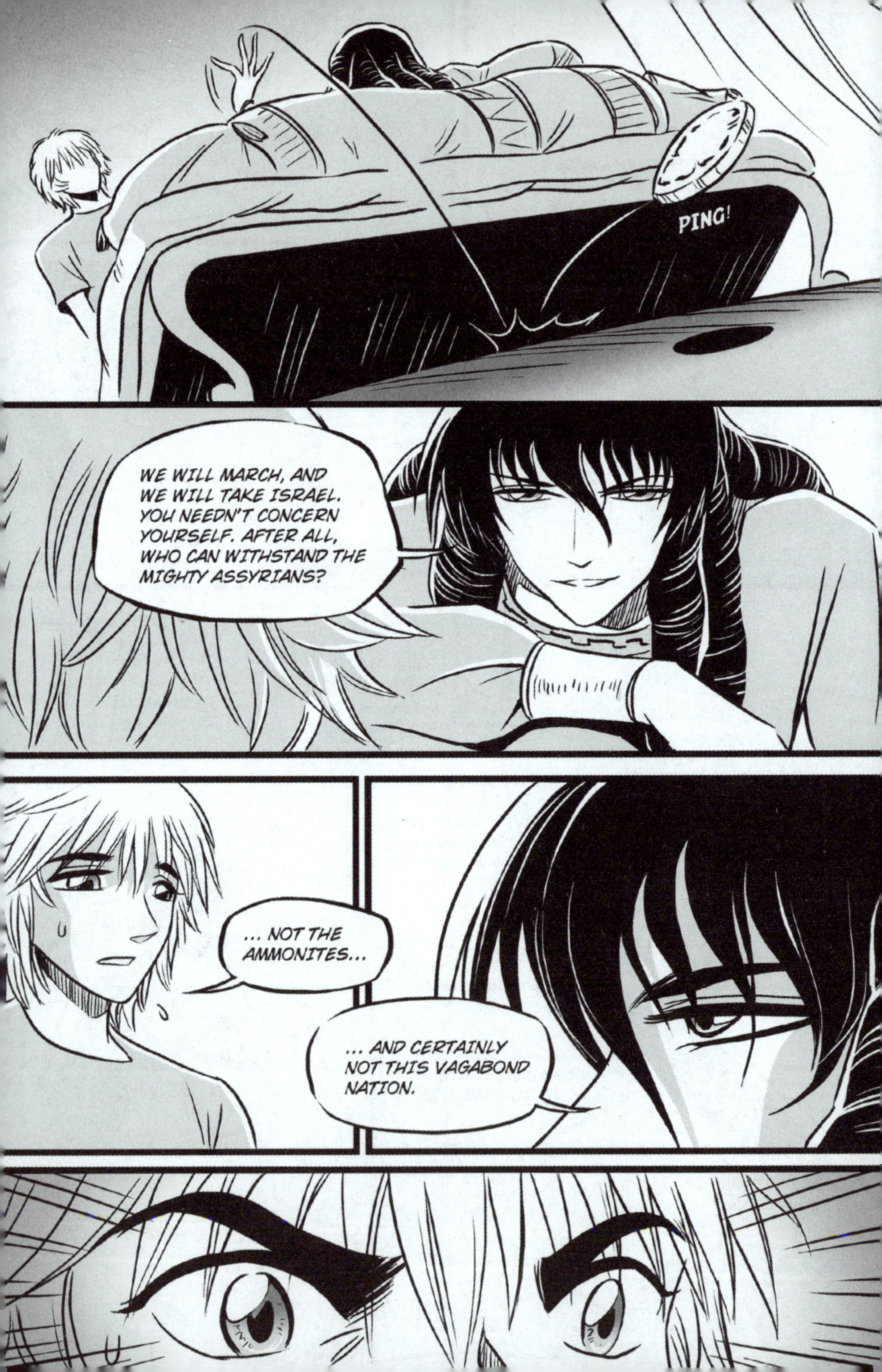

PING!
WE WILL MARCH, AND WE WILL TAKE ISRAEL. YOU NEEDN'T CONCERN YOURSELF. AFTER ALL, WHO CAN WITHSTAND THE MIGHTY ASSYRIANS?
... NOT THE AMMONITES...
... AND CERTAINLY NOT THIS VAGABOND NATION.

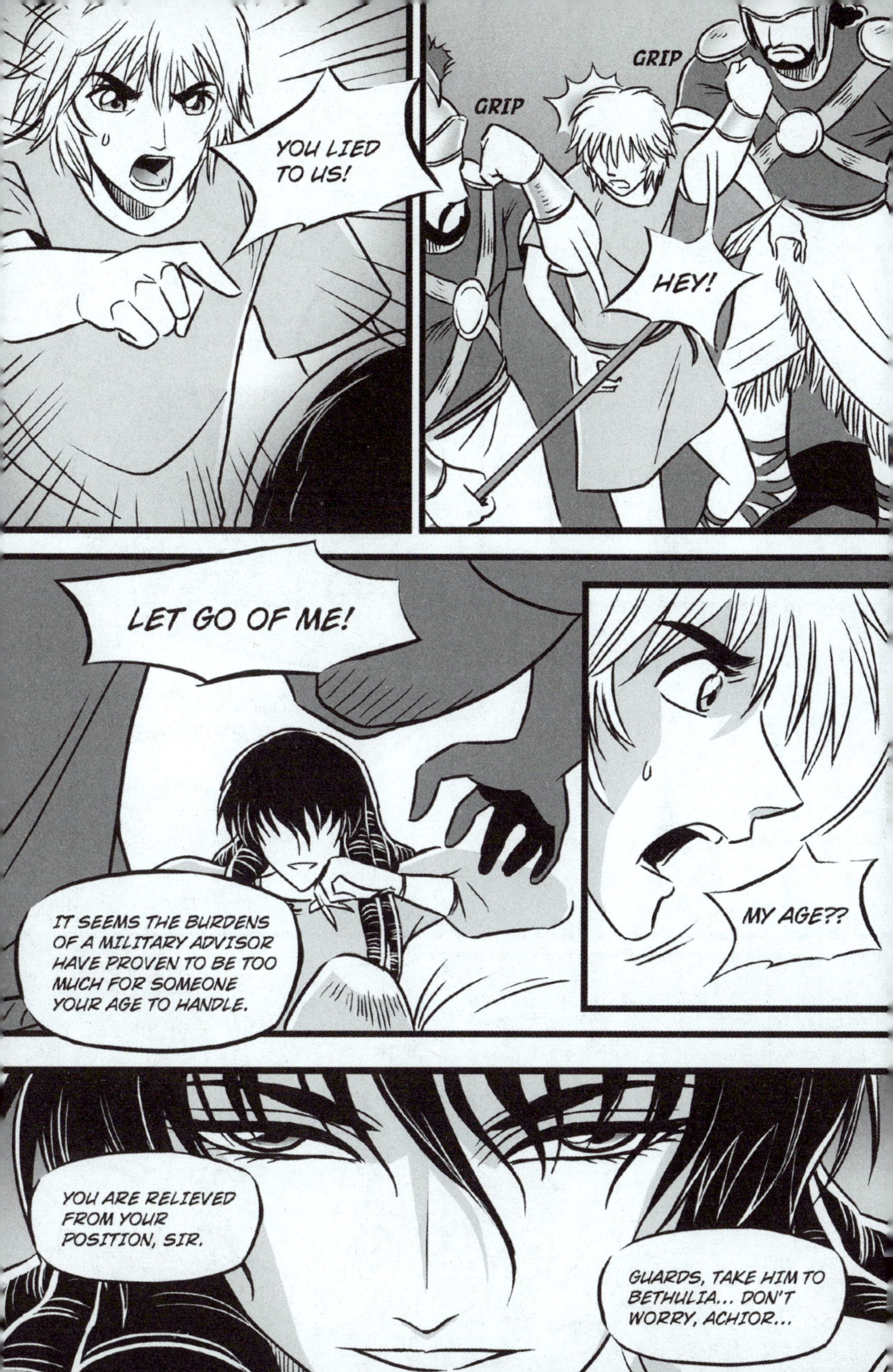
YOU LIED TO US!
GRIP
GRIP
HEY!
LET GO OF ME!
IT SEEMS THE BURDENS OF A MILITARY ADVISOR HAVE PROVEN TO BE TOO MUCH FOR SOMEONE YOUR AGE TO HANDLE.
MY AGE??
YOU ARE RELIEVED FROM YOUR POSITION, SIR.
GUARDS, TAKE HIM TO BETHULIA... DON'T WORRY, ACHIOR...

YOU'LL SEE YOUR SOLDIERS AGAIN SOON.
YOU CAN'T DO THAT! YOU CAN'T JUST LIE, AND CHEAT, AND USE EVERYONE!
YOU DON'T OWN EVERYTHING!!
... SOON ENOUGH.

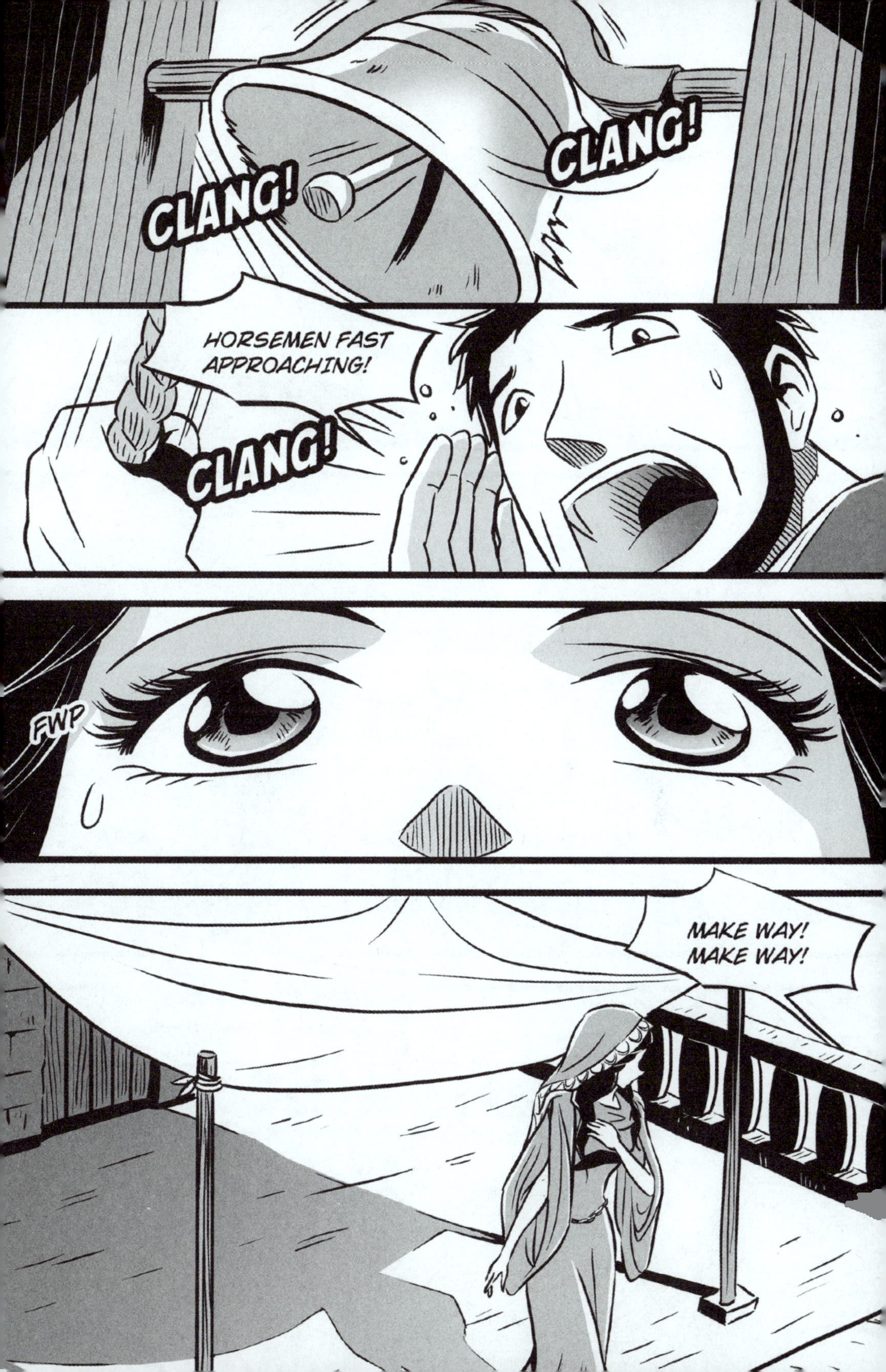
CLANG!
CLANG!
CLANG!
HORSEMEN FAST APPROACHING!
FWP
MAKE WAY! MAKE WAY!

WHAT?
THIS NEWS MUST REACH THE ELDERS!
GALLOP
GALLOP
MESSAGE FOR THE ELDERS! MAKE WAY!
GALLOP
GALLOP

JUDITH!
IS IT HOLOFERNES?
TAP
TAP
NO IT'S OUR MEN – THEY HAVE A PRISONER.
APPARENTLY THERE WAS A SKIRMISH AT THE NARROW WAY.
TAP
TAP
TAP

THEY'RE TAKING HIM TO THE ELDERS.
NO, MY LADY! I'LL GO! YOU NEED TO STAY HERE IN CASE THERE'S AN ATTACK!
I'LL BE BACK!
BUT...
SHFF

CREAK
ZUSA!
OH GOD...
DON'T LET ANYTHING HAPPEN TO HER.

TSSSS
DO YOU REALLY THINK THAT GUY WAS RULER OF THE AMMONITES?
PFFT. HOW SHOULD I KNOW?

THEY'RE PROBABLY IN BETHULIA BY NOW.
PROBABLY. IT'S ONLY A FEW MILES THAT WAY.
TCK
PHEW!
GEEZ IT'S HOT... AND ALL THIS COPPER DOESN'T HELP... HEY, WHEN IS OUR SHIFT UP?
WE HAVE ANOTHER THREE HOURS YET.
SIGH...
THREE HOURS?... HEY, GIMME SOME OF YOUR WATER.
HAHAHA!
WITH THE WAY YOU'VE BEEN GUZZLING, YOU'LL BE UP ALL NIGHT.
SHHHHT!

SHUNK!
AARON!
THUMP
WE'RE UNDER ATTACK!
SHIELDS UP!
CHINK
CHINK
CHINK
GRAB
UGH... IT'S TOO DARK...

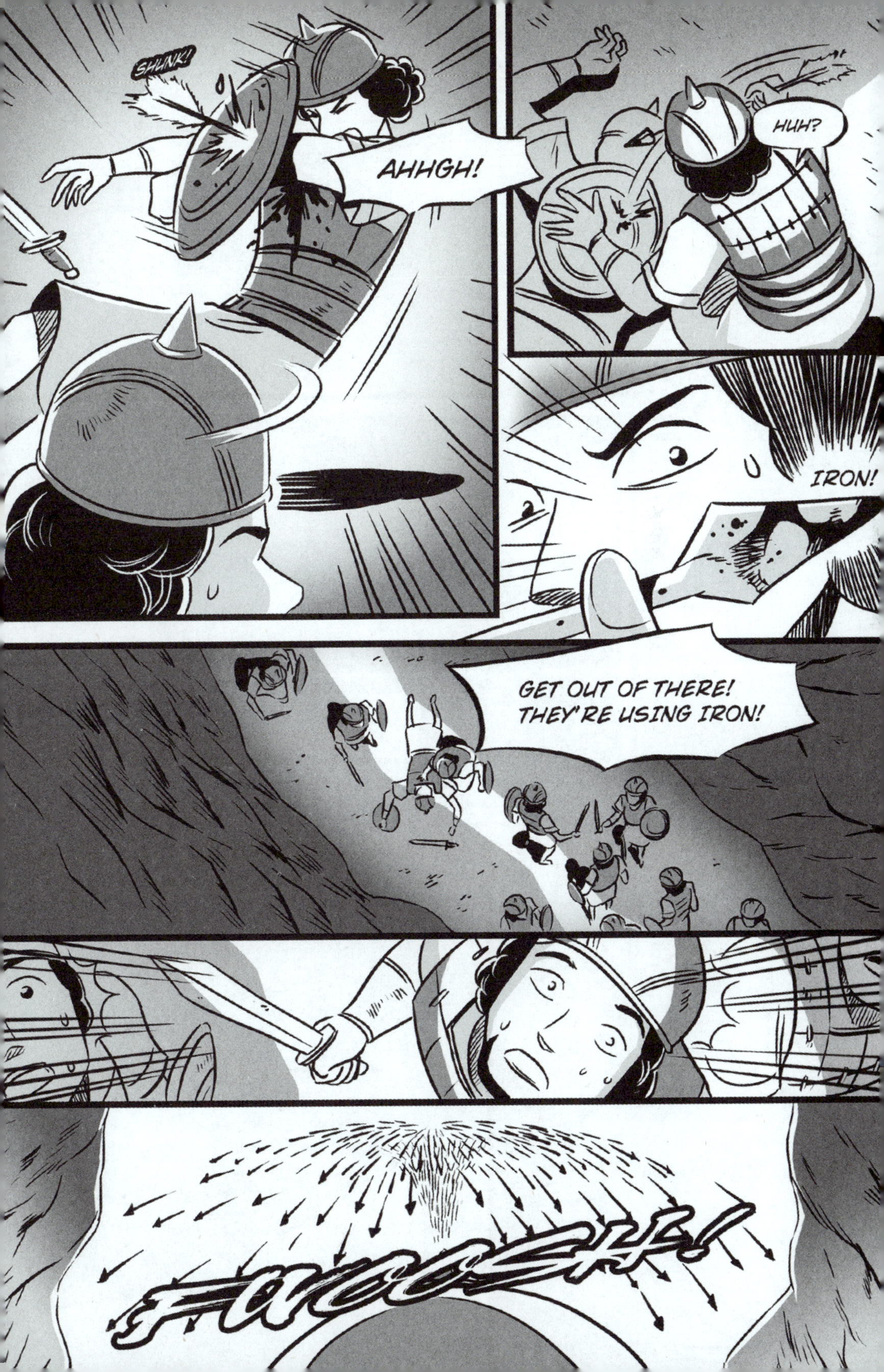

SHUNK!
AHHGH!
HUH?
IRON!
GET OUT OF THERE! THEY'RE USING IRON!
FWOOSH!

AHH!
AHH!
UGH!
PING!
PING!
PING!
TROMP
TROMP
TROMP
TROMP
TROMP

SHIVER
WELL THAT WAS DISAPPOINTING.
MY, MY, AREN'T YOU THE FORTUNATE ONE?
GO AHEAD AND KILL ME! BUT YOU'LL NEVER BE ABLE TO BEAT ALL OF ISRAEL!
OH WE DON'T WANT TO FIGHT ALL OF ISRAEL... JUST JERUSALEM.
JERUSALEM?

AFTER ALL...
IF YOU WANT SOMETHING DEAD...
SHINK
YOU HAVE TO CUT OFF ITS HEAD.
CLASH!
SLICE
YOU LOSE.

MY LADY!
HOLOFERNES! HOLOFERNES' ARMY IS COMING!
DOOON
LOOK AT THE SIZE OF THEM...

WHAT DO
WE DO?

ZUSA, WHERE
ARE YOU?

MMMPH...
MURMUR
MURMUR
MURMUR
I CAN'T SEE A THING!
OOF!

AH! MUCH BETTER.
OOHH
RUB RUB
HE'S KINDA CUTE.

WHO ARE YOU?
WHAT? OH, I'M ACHIOR. LEADER OF THE AMMONITES.
HOW DO WE KNOW YOU'RE NOT JUST A SPY FOR HOLOFERNES?
WELL, I DON'T KNOW... HOW DO WE KNOW YOU'RE NOT ONE?

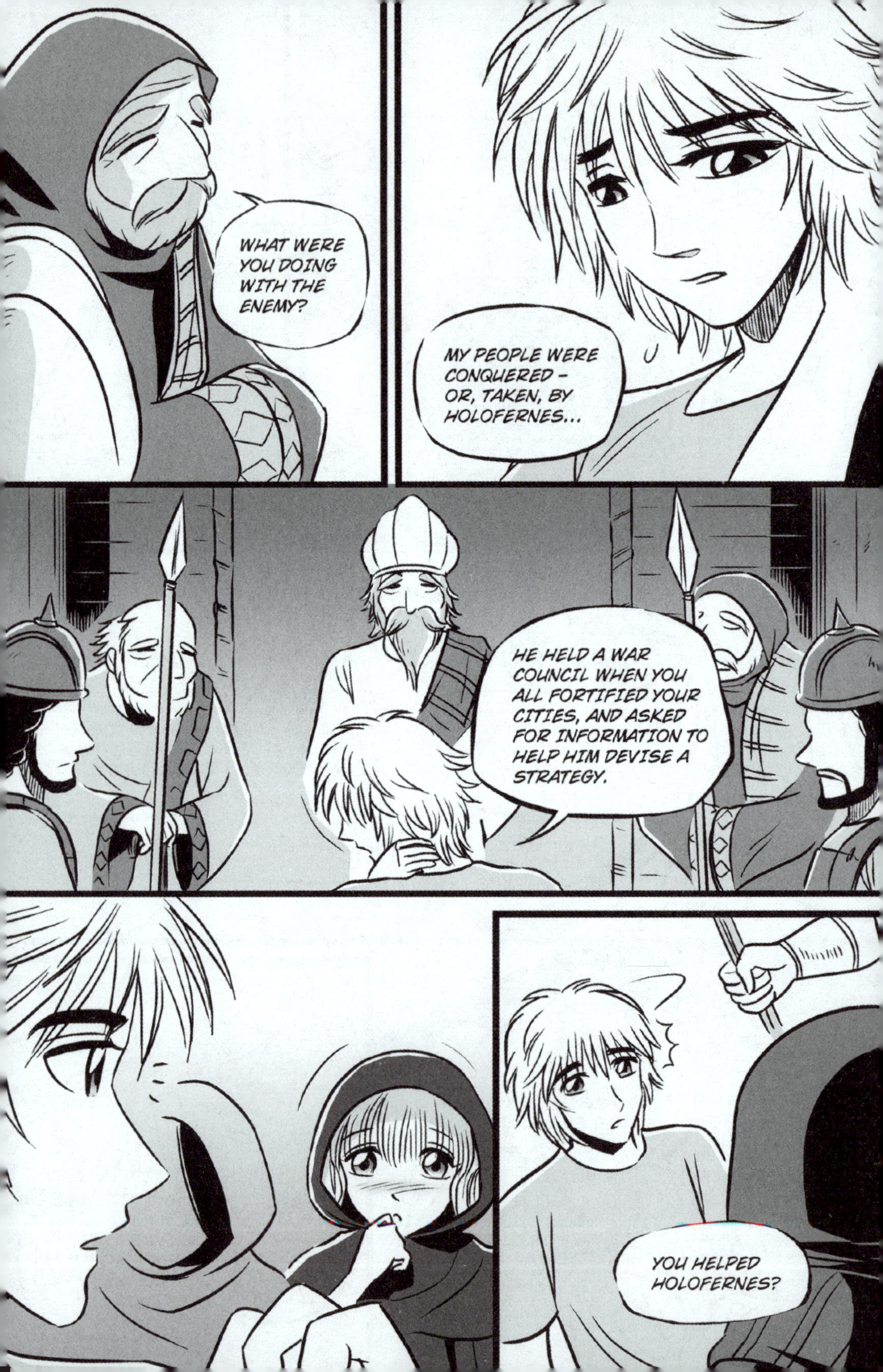

WHAT WERE YOU DOING WITH THE ENEMY?
MY PEOPLE WERE CONQUERED — OR, TAKEN, BY HOLOFERNES...
HE HELD A WAR COUNCIL WHEN YOU ALL FORTIFIED YOUR CITIES, AND ASKED FOR INFORMATION TO HELP HIM DEVISE A STRATEGY.
YOU HELPED HOLOFERNES?

WHAT? NO! WELL, NOT REALLY.
I HEARD ALL ABOUT HOW YOU GUYS WORSHIP A GOD THAT CAN'T BE CONQUERED...
AND SINCE HOLOFERNES HAS DRAFTED ALL MY MEN INTO HIS ARMY, I DIDN'T REALLY WANT THEM TO FIGHT YOU IF THE RUMORS WERE TRUE.
SO I TOLD HIM NOT TO ATTACK YOU GUYS... NEXT THING I KNOW, HERE I AM.
THAT'S WHAT I GET FOR OPENING MY BIG MOUTH, HUH?
GRIN

WAIT, SO IS HE GOING TO ATTACK?
YES. NOW THAT HIS PRIDE'S BEEN WOUNDED, THERE'S NOTHING THAT'S GOING TO STOP HIM FROM COMING. AND I'M REALLY HOPING THIS GOD OF YOURS UPHOLDS HIS REPUTATION.
MURMUR
BUT WE'VE BEEN PRAYING SO HARD!
MAYBE WE'RE NOT PRAYING ENOUGH!
MURMUR
MURMUR
MAYBE WE SHOULD SURRENDER NOW... HE MIGHT HAVE MERCY ON US...
NO! YOU CAN'T SURRENDER! YOU DON'T KNOW THIS GUY. HE'S DANGEROUS! HE WILL DESTROY YOU!

CHATTER
CHATTER
CHATTER
CHATTER
HE'LL DESECRATE THE TEMPLE!
HE'LL KILL OUR MEN AND TAKE OUR WOMEN!
PLEASE, EVERYONE! WE ARE PLENTY FORTIFIED!
WHEN HE COMES WE WILL BE ABLE TO SURVIVE LONG ENOUGH FOR JERUSALEM TO SEND US REINFORCEMENTS!
HUFF
HUFF
SHOVE

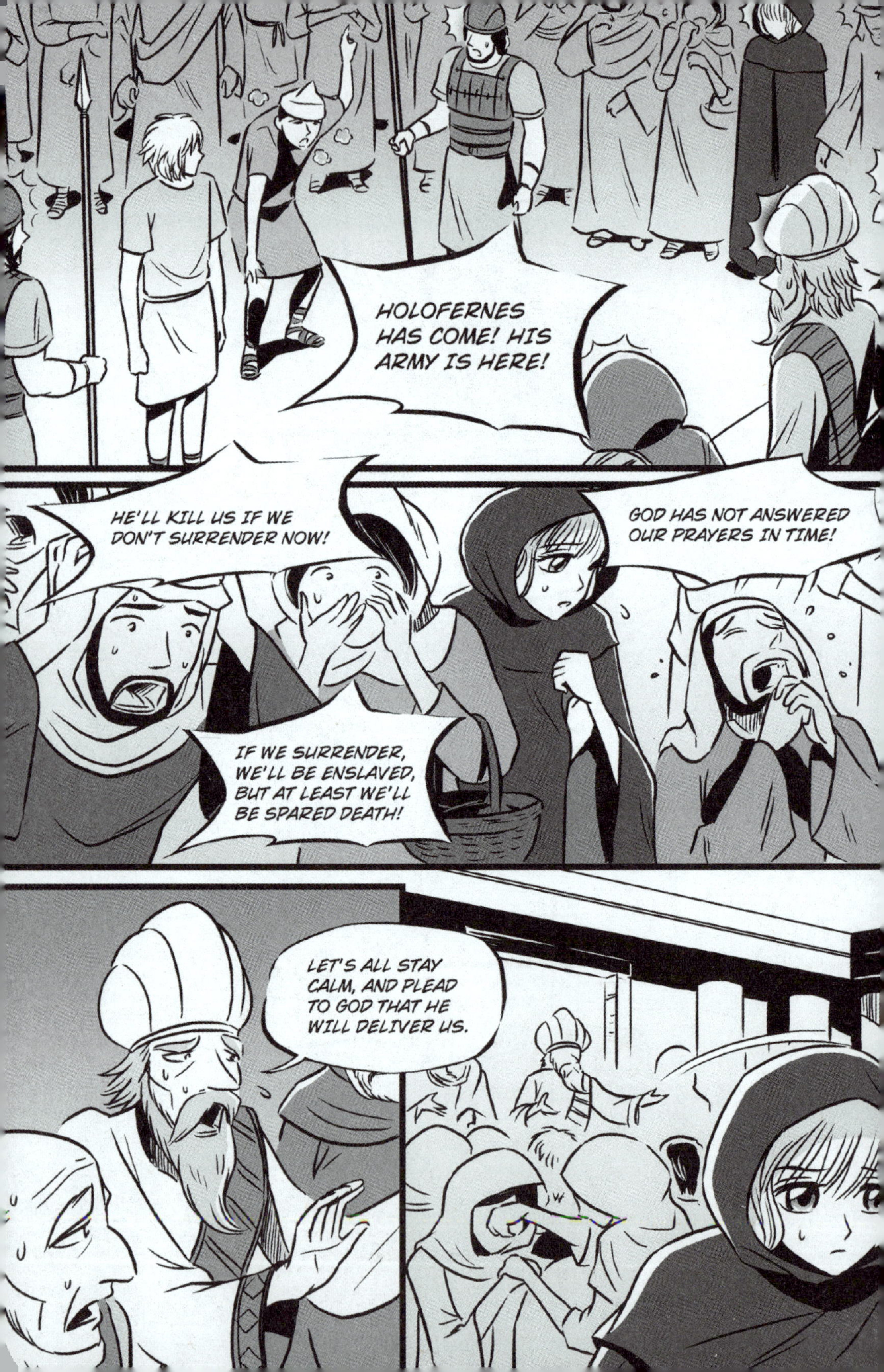

HOLOFERNES HAS COME! HIS ARMY IS HERE!
HE'LL KILL US IF WE DON'T SURRENDER NOW!
GOD HAS NOT ANSWERED OUR PRAYERS IN TIME!
IF WE SURRENDER, WE'LL BE ENSLAVED, BUT AT LEAST WE'LL BE SPARED DEATH!
LET'S ALL STAY CALM, AND PLEAD TO GOD THAT HE WILL DELIVER US.

SO THEN I RACED BACK HERE TO SEE IF YOU WERE ALRIGHT.
JUDITH?
I UNDERSTAND HOW YOU CONDUCT YOURSELF IN A WAY FITTING FOR A HANDMAIDEN... AND YOUR FIDELITY AND CONCERN FOR MY SAFETY ARE COMMENDABLE... BUT ZUSA...

NEVER DO SOMETHING LIKE THAT AGAIN.
I... I DON'T UNDERSTAND, MY LADY—
I'VE ASKED YOU NOT TO CALL ME THAT!
SORRY, JUDITH...

PLEASE UNDER-STAND, ZUSA... I'M ALL ALONE IN THE WORLD.
FOR A REASON UNKNOWN TO ME, GOD HAS DENIED ME A LONG LIFE WITH MY HUSBAND, AND DENIED ME EVEN A CHILD BY HIM.
YOU ARE... MORE THAN A HANDMAIDEN TO ME, ZUSA... TREAT ME LESS LIKE ROYALTY, AND MORE LIKE...
SIGH
... SO TELL ME MORE ABOUT THIS ACHIOR.

CLACK
CLACK
THEY HAVE FORTIFIED THEMSELVES, MY LORD.
OH, BUT IT'S ALL THE MORE FUN WHEN THEY DO.

THIS CITY IS DESIGNED TO WITHSTAND LONG-TERM SIEGES. WHO KNOWS HOW LONG THEY ARE CAPABLE OF LASTING IN THERE?
WE SHOULD SAVE TIME AND JUST MOVE ON TO JERUSALEM.
NO. THROUGH THEIR DISOBEDIENCE THEY HAVE SHOWN GREAT DISRESPECT. WHEN THEY FORTIFIED THEMSELVES, THEY ASKED FOR A SIEGE... WHY SHOULD I DENY IT TO THEM?
WE'LL WAIT THEM OUT.
MY LORD! THAT COULD TAKE MONTHS! SURELY THEY WILL HAVE STOCKPILED PLENTY OF PROVISIONS PRIOR TO OUR COMING?

MONTHS? I'D SAY ONE... MAYBE TWO WEEKS AT THE VERY MOST.
SHRUG
WHAT IS IT YOU PLAN TO DO, MY LORD?
- TAKE YOUR MEN TO THE BASE OF THE CITY. FIND THE SOURCE OF THEIR WATER, AND CUT IT OFF... CHANNEL IT TO OUR TROOPS INSTEAD.
THE REST OF YOU... TAKE YOUR TROOPS AND USE THE SURROUNDING MOUNTAINTOPS AS VANTAGE POINTS. STOP AND REPORT ANYONE WHO TRIES TO FLEE THE CITY.

AND YOU...
PREPARE THE BIGGEST HERBAL BATH POSSIBLE IN MY TENT.
WE CAN'T LET THE WATER GO TO WASTE NOW, CAN WE?

BRUSSHH
BETHULIA... 3 DAYS MARCH TO-
KOHEN GADOL!
KOHEN GADOL!
BAM!
BETHULIA IS SURROUNDED, AND THE ENEMY OCCUPIES ALL THE HIGH GROUND! ANY BACKUP WE SEND CAN'T GET THROUGH! WE CAN'T EVEN GET A MESSAGE TO THEM!
OH LORD, I HOPE THEY KNOW WHAT TO DO...

CAW!
CAW!
TSSSS
TSSSS
SQUEAK
HOW LONG HAS IT BEEN?

THE PEOPLE NEED WATER SOON...
MANY PEOPLE ARE PRAYING FOR DELIVERANCE...
BUT I WISH THE ELDERS WOULD HURRY UP AND DO SOMETHING.

KNOCK
KNOCK
CREEEAK
PANT
PANT
HEY... DOES JUDITH LIVE HERE?
THUD

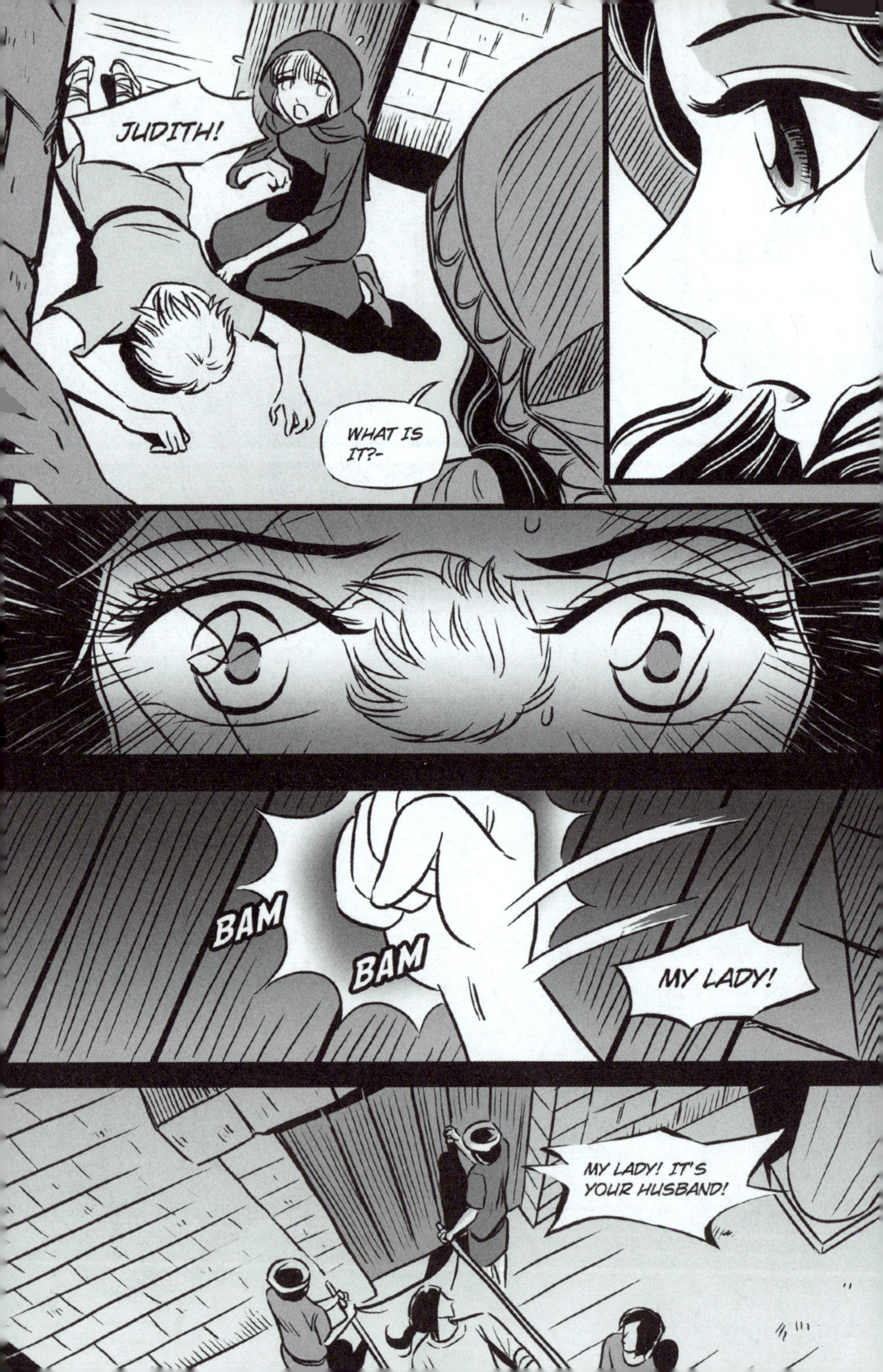
JUDITH!
WHAT IS IT?-
BAM
BAM
MY LADY!
MY LADY! IT'S YOUR HUSBAND!

WHAT'S WRONG?
MANASSEH?!
MANASSEH!

WHAT
HAPPENED?

HE COLLAPSED FROM
DEHYDRATION.

HE WAS LYING
THERE FOR SOME
TIME BEFORE
ANYONE FOUND HIM.

I DON'T KNOW IF HE'S GOING TO MAKE IT...
OH, GOD...
PLEASE LET HIM BE ALRIGHT.

JUDITH...
WHY WOULD I KEEP SILENT WHEN MY LAST DAY ON THIS EARTH COULD BE SPENT TALKING TO YOU?
DON'T TALK... SAVE YOUR STRENGTH.
STOP NOW – DON'T TALK LIKE THAT.
YOU HAVE TO BE OPEN TO WHATEVER HAPPENS TO ME. DO YOU UNDERSTAND?... NOTHING HAPPENS WITHOUT REASON.
NO, LISTEN TO ME...

STOP IT! DON'T SAY THAT!...
NO! YOU CAN'T DIE!
YOU'RE GOING TO BE ALRIGHT. YOU HAVE TO BE...
JUDITH, LISTEN... I AM GOING TO—
SQUEEZE
WE ALL HAVE A ROLE TO PLAY IN THIS LIFE. WHETHER IT'S MARCHING OFF TO BATTLE OR SIMPLY HARVESTING GRAIN.
SO LONG AS WE PERFORM AT OUR BEST, THAT'S ALL THAT REALLY MATTERS.

I HAVE NO REGRETS, WITH ONLY ONE EXCEPTION...
I DID MY PART FOR ISRAEL... I MARRIED THE MOST BEAUTIFUL WOMAN IN THE WORLD, PROVIDED FOR HER, AND FED MY PEOPLE.
I'M SORRY WE COULD NOT HAVE ANY CHILDREN.
... WHAT AM I SUPPOSED TO DO WHEN YOU'RE GONE?
YOU HAVE A PART TO PLAY TOO, THAT GOD WILL HELP YOU WITH...
AND I SUPPOSE THERE'S A REASON FOR THAT TOO...

YOU JUST CAN'T SIT BACK AND HOPE SOMEONE ELSE IS GOING TO DO IT FOR YOU... BE THE STRONG, RESOURCEFUL WOMAN I'VE ALWAYS LOVED...
I DON'T KNOW IF I CAN WITHOUT YOU.
... JUST BE YOU.
TRIALS ARE SENT TO STRENGTHEN US, AND FORCE US TO DO OUR PART. YOU'VE LED A GOOD LIFE – A LIFE IN THE LIGHT – AND IT'S TREATED YOU WELL.
BUT...
IT'S ONLY IN THE DARK THAT YOU CAN SEE THE STARS...

BUT, MANASSEH...
MANASSEH?

MANASSEH! MANASSEH,
DON'T LEAVE ME!

PERISH THE THOUGHT...

MANASSEH!... MANASSEH?...
WHY, GOD?
I WILL NEVER LOVE ANOTHER.
YOU ARE A JEALOUS GOD, RIGHT? WAS THAT WHY YOU TOOK HIM? SO I WOULD CONSECRATE MYSELF TO YOU?

I JUST WANT TO KNOW...
... SO THIS IS ACHIOR?
BRUSH
MM-HMM.
AND HE SAID HE'S THE LEADER OF THE AMMONITES?
THAT'S WHAT HE SAID.

HE'S KIND OF YOUNG, ISN'T HE?
I JUST THINK HE HAS A BABY-FACE.
OH! HE'S UP!
HEY, WHO ARE YOU CALLING A BABY-FACE?
HEY? DIDN'T I SEE YOU AT THE ELDERS'?
SHUFF

YES, THAT WAS ME.
OH – SO DOES THAT MAKE YOU JUDITH?
IT DOES... AND WHAT BRINGS YOU HERE, ACHIOR OF THE AMMONITES?
AH, SO YOU KNOW ME ALREADY?... NOT SURE IF THAT'S A GOOD THING OR A BAD THING!
YOU CAME HERE SEEKING ME BY NAME... WHY IS THAT?

THE PEOPLE SPEAK HIGHLY OF YOU, AND I HEARD YOU HOLD A LOT OF LEEWAY IN THIS CITY... SO I THOUGHT YOU MIGHT BE ABLE TO CHANGE THE ELDERS' MINDS.
CHANGE THEIR MINDS?
YEAH, LAST NIGHT THEY HAD A MEETING WITH SOME OF THE TOWNSPEOPLE WHO WERE CLOSE TO RIOTING... THEY WERE YELLING AT THE ELDERS FOR NOT SURRENDERING WHEN THEY HAD THE CHANCE. THEY LOOKED LIKE THEY WERE READY TO STONE THE ELDERS!... HAHA!
BUT I THINK THEY'RE ALL JUST SCARED.
SO WHAT DID THE ELDERS DO?

THEY CAME TO A COMPROMISE: IF IN 5 DAYS YOUR GOD DOES NOT DELIVER THEM...
THEY WOULD SURRENDER THE CITY.
WHAT??
THAT'S WHAT THEY TOLD THE PEOPLE. SO NOW EVERYONE IS PRAYING LIKE CRAZY. NOT LIKE IT WILL DO ANY GOOD.
WHAT DO YOU MEAN BY THAT?

JUST THAT ALL THE TOWNSPEOPLE ARE BEGINNING TO THINK YOUR GOD'S ABANDONED THEM.
IT'S A GOOD THING HE DOESN'T GIVE UP ON US AS EASILY AS WE DO ON HIM.
SCOFF
WOW, YOU REALLY BELIEVE IN THIS GOD DON'T YOU?
SIP
IF WE SURRENDER, THERE WILL BE NOTHING KEEPING HOLOFERNES FROM DEFILING THE SANCTUARY IN JERUSALEM.
NOT REALLY. I GAVE UP ON MILCOM WHEN MY PRAYER TO SAVE MY CITY WENT UNANSWERED.
DON'T THE AMMONITES HAVE A GOD THEY PRAY TO?
MAYBE THE ANSWER WAS "NO."

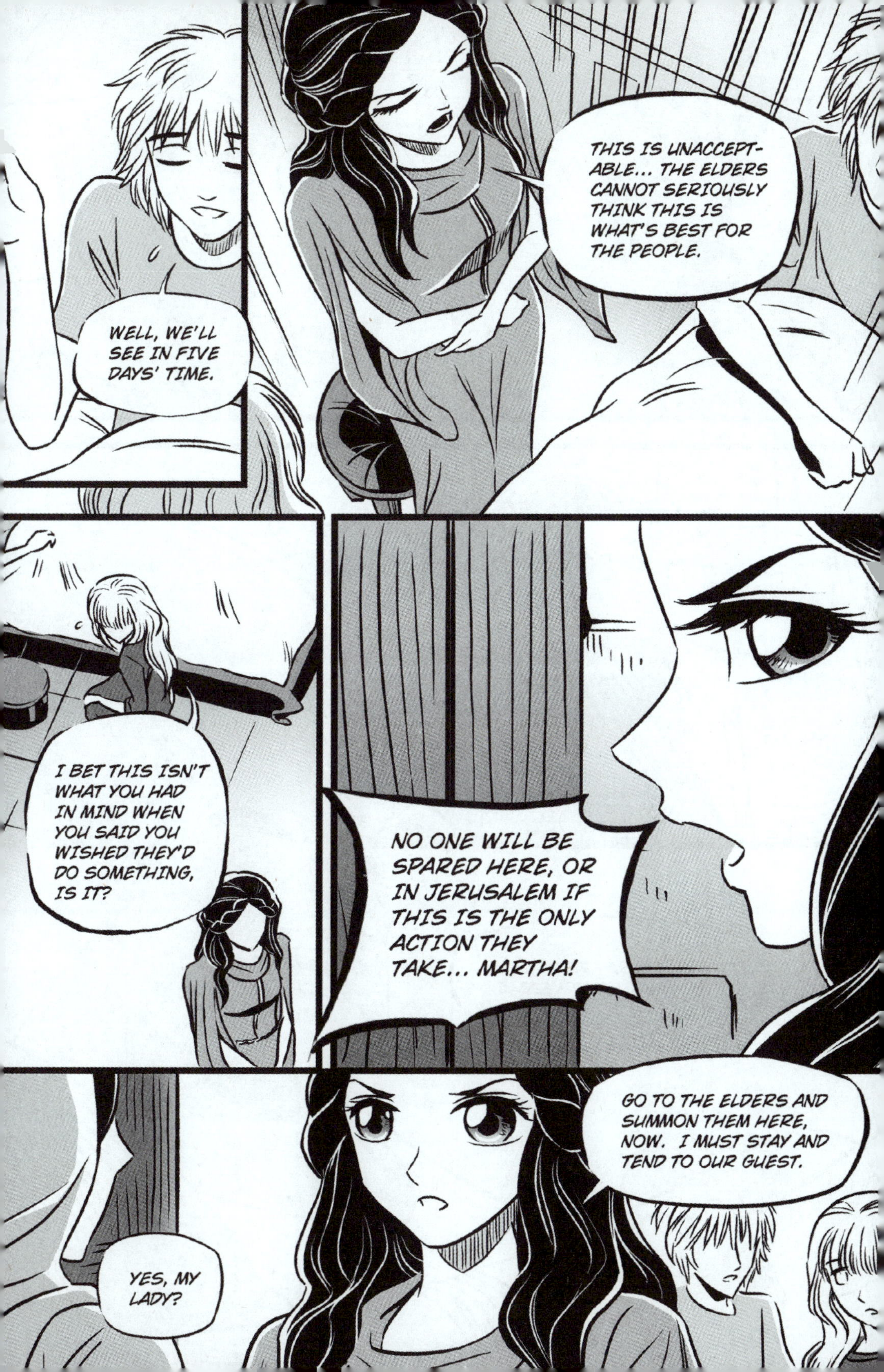
THIS IS UNACCEPTABLE... THE ELDERS CANNOT SERIOUSLY THINK THIS IS WHAT'S BEST FOR THE PEOPLE.
WELL, WE'LL SEE IN FIVE DAYS' TIME.
I BET THIS ISN'T WHAT YOU HAD IN MIND WHEN YOU SAID YOU WISHED THEY'D DO SOMETHING, IS IT?
NO ONE WILL BE SPARED HERE, OR IN JERUSALEM IF THIS IS THE ONLY ACTION THEY TAKE... MARTHA!
GO TO THE ELDERS AND SUMMON THEM HERE, NOW. I MUST STAY AND TEND TO OUR GUEST.
YES, MY LADY?

MY LORD...
BRUSSHH
SIGH
WHAT IS IT
THIS TIME,
BAGOAS?
A MESSAGE FROM
KING NEBUCHADNEZZAR.

WHAT DOES IT SAY?
I... DID NOT OPEN IT.
KNIFE ON THE TABLE.
I BELIEVE IT IS FOR YOUR EYES ALONE, MY LORD.
HONESTLY BAGOAS, I CAN'T DO EVERYTHING AROUND HERE MYSELF... OPEN THE SCROLL AND TELL ME WHAT IT SAYS.

HIS MAJESTY ORDERS THAT YOU WASTE NO TIME WITH BETHULIA, AND PRESS ON TO JERUSALEM.
BRUSH
MY LORD...?
YES, BAGOAS?
WHAT ARE YOUR ORDERS?
BURN IT.

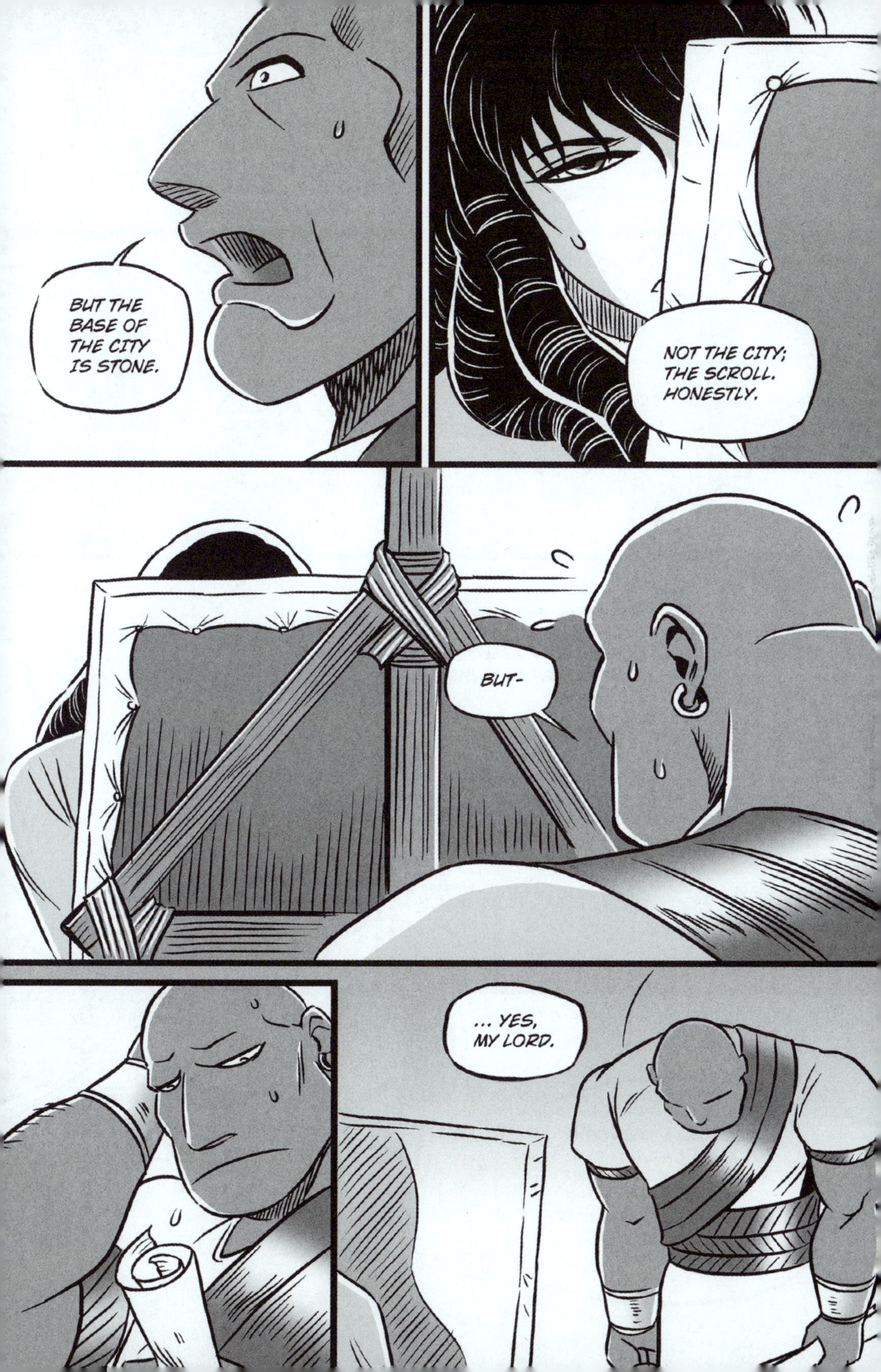

BUT THE BASE OF THE CITY IS STONE.
NOT THE CITY; THE SCROLL. HONESTLY.
BUT—
...YES, MY LORD.

WELCOME, EVERYONE. FORGIVE ME FOR NOT COMING TO YOU MYSELF, BUT I COULD NOT LEAVE MY GUEST.
OH, CERTAINLY... WHAT CAN WE DO FOR YOU, JUDITH?
SQUIRM
I CALL YOU HERE TODAY BECAUSE I HEARD THAT YOU AGREED TO SURRENDER TO HOLOFERNES IF THE PEOPLE'S PRAYERS WERE NOT ANSWERED IN FIVE DAYS' TIME.

TELL ME: IS THIS TRUE?
UH... YES... MY LADY.
THAT IS UNACCEPTABLE. THE WORKS OF HEAVEN ARE INSCRUTABLE... I CERTAINLY HOPE YOU DO NOT ACTUALLY PLAN TO GO THROUGH WITH THIS?
MY LADY, IT IS A DIFFICULT SITUATION...
I DON'T SEE WHY IT IS. SIMPLY CHANGE YOUR PLAN.

UNFORTUNATELY WE CANNOT.
YOU WOULD RISK THE DESECRATION OF THE TEMPLE, AND THE DESTRUCTION OF ISRAEL?
... ALL OUR MEN WILL BE KILLED, AND KNOWING THE ASSYRIANS THEY WILL SHAME OUR WOMEN AS WELL.
NO-WELL, YOU SEE...
WE HAVE ALREADY SWORN TO THE PEOPLE, UNDER OATH, THAT WE WOULD.

NOD

... YOU... HAVE SWORN UNDER SACRED OATH?

WHY WOULD YOU DO SUCH A THING? YOU KNOW WE'RE THE ONLY THING BETWEEN HOLOFERNES AND THE HOLY CITY!

THEY WERE SERIOUSLY READY TO STONE US OTHERWISE...

DID YOU HONESTLY THINK HOLOFERNES WOULD BE ANY MORE MERCIFUL TO ALL OF ISRAEL?

... WE CAN'T GO BACK ON OUR WORD...
AND WE CAN'T WAIT ON GOD FOREVER.
CHUCKLE
CHUCKLE
UNBELIEVABLE. YOU ARE SO QUICK TO PUT A TIME LIMIT ON GOD'S WORKS WHEN YOU ARE ALL MORE THAN CONTENT TO SIT INACTIVE?
WHAT WOULD YOU HAVE US DO?
...

FIVE DAYS...
I WONDER WHAT'S GOING TO HAPPEN TO ALL OF US.
WE'LL BE FINE.
HOW CAN YOU BE SO SURE?
BECAUSE I KNOW WHAT WE HAVE TO DO IN ORDER TO SURVIVE... I KNOW WHAT I HAVE TO DO...
I'M JUST SCARED TO DO IT.

WHAT DO YOU MEAN?
...
JUDITH?
WHAT ARE YOU PLANNING TO DO?
I'M GOING TO KILL HOLOFERNES.

ZUSA, WHAT IF... THIS IS WHY HE DIED? AND WHY WE HAD NO CHILDREN?...
... ARE YOU SERIOUS?...
SHIFF
I FEEL LIKE THIS IS WHAT I'M CALLED TO DO... LIKE THIS IS MY PART TO PLAY IN THE DEFENSE OF ISRAEL.
... ARE YOU SURE?
NOD
WELL... IF ANYONE CAN FIGURE OUT A WAY TO PULL THAT OFF, IT WOULD BE YOU...

DO THE ELDERS
KNOW?

NOT REALLY.

I TOLD THEM I HAD A
PLAN, AND ASKED THEIR
PERMISSION TO LEAVE
THE CITY.

... WHEN?

I LEAVE
TONIGHT.

I KNOW YOU FEEL RESPONSIBLE FOR OTHERS...
BUT... OTHERS CARE ABOUT YOU TOO YOU KNOW.
SHFF
I KNOW IT'S GOING TO BE VERY DANGEROUS, ZUSA... I WILL BE IN THE MIDDLE OF AN ARMY OF 120 THOUSAND ENEMY SOLDIERS AT LEAST...
AND I WILL HAVE TO MEET AND DECEIVE A DANGEROUS MAN THAT HAS CONQUERED WHOLE NATIONS, WHO IS ALSO AN INFAMOUS WOMANIZER...
...THE MAN THAT I PLAN TO KILL.

OF COURSE IT'S GOING TO BE DANGEROUS...
... SO I COMPLETELY UNDERSTAND IF YOU REFUSE WHEN I ASK YOU TO COME WITH ME.
... JUST THIS ONCE.

OH GOD...
YOU HAVE DESIGNED THE THINGS THAT ARE NOW, AND THOSE THAT ARE TO COME...
HERE NOW ARE THE ASSYRIANS, WHICH NUMBER AMONG THE THOUSANDS...
FSHHT
THIS IS THE LAST OF IT.

THEY DO NOT KNOW THAT YOU ARE THE LORD WHO CRUSHES WARS...
RUSTLE
CLASP

BREAK THEIR STRENGTH BY YOUR MIGHT, AND BRING DOWN THEIR POWER IN YOUR ANGER...
FOR THEY INTEND TO DEFILE YOUR SANCTUARY...
LOOK AT THEIR PRIDE AND SEND YOUR WRATH...
GIVE TO ME, YOUR HANDMAIDEN, A WIDOW, THE STRONG HAND TO DO WHAT I PLAN.

LOOK!
CRACKLE
HERE SHE COMES.

WOAH...
HEY, YOUR MOUTH IS OPEN.
SHE'S BEAUTIFUL!
SHE HASN'T DRESSED LIKE THAT SINCE...
PLEASE ORDER THE GATE OPENED.
OH! YES! CERTAINLY.
OPEN THE GATES!

GRIIIIND
... GOD BE WITH YOU.
GRIIIIND
IT'S REALLY DARK OUT THERE...
THAT'S ALRIGHT...

THE STARS WILL SHINE ALL THE BRIGHTER BECAUSE OF IT.

"FOR NOW IS THE TIME TO HELP YOUR INHERITANCE, AND TO CARRY OUT MY UNDERTAKING FOR THE DESTRUCTION OF THE ENEMIES WHO HAVE RISEN UP AGAINST US." - JUDITH 13:5

GOOD MORNING, BEAUTIFUL.
HOW DID YOU SLEEP?

WELL ENOUGH... YOURSELF?
I GOT TO SLEEP NEXT TO THE MOST BEAUTIFUL WOMAN IN THE WORLD. I DIDN'T SLEEP A WINK.
OH PLEASE.
SORRY, AM I MAKING IT HARD FOR YOU TO STAY HUMBLE?
YOU'RE RIDICULOUS.

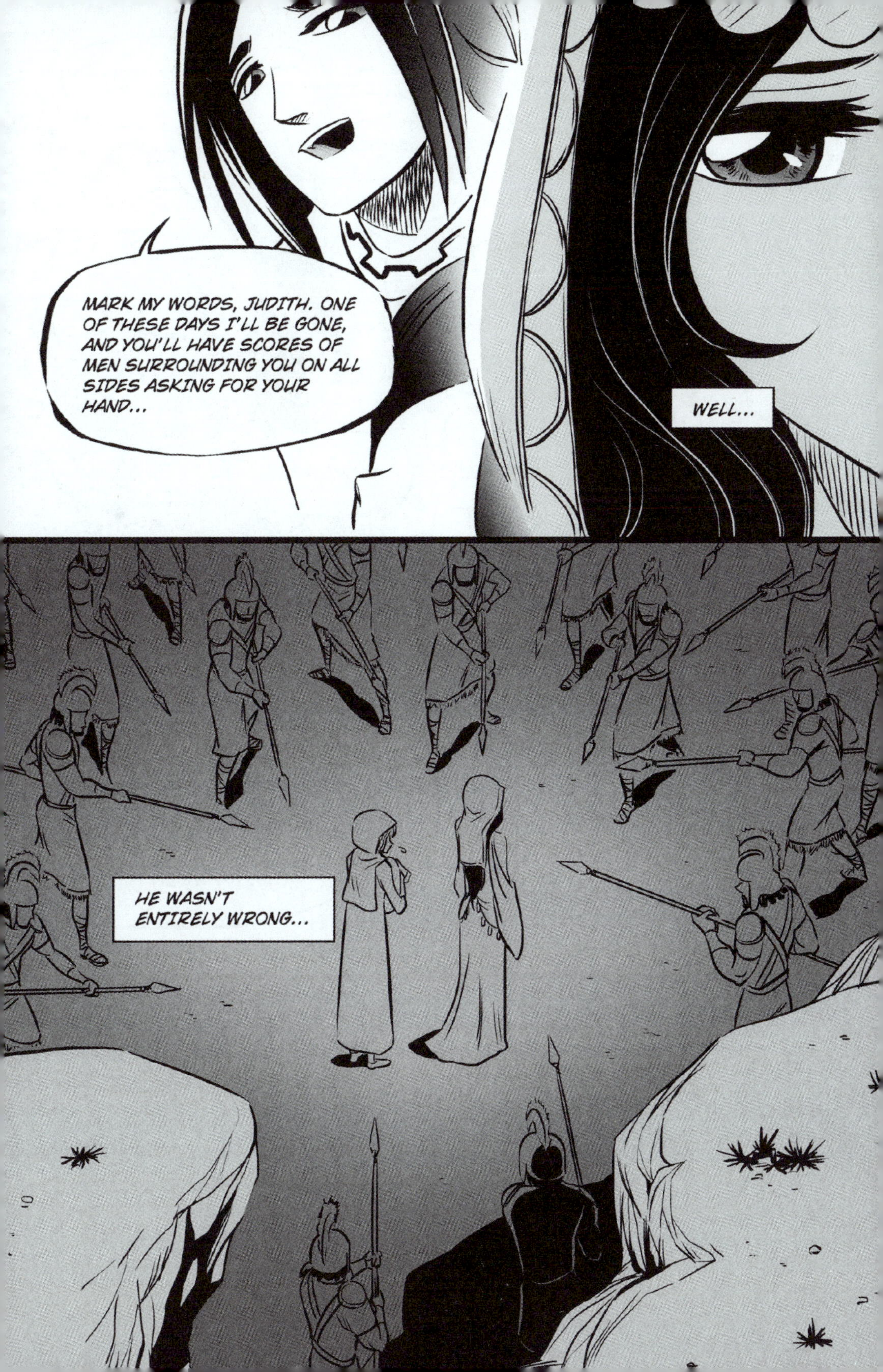

MARK MY WORDS, JUDITH. ONE OF THESE DAYS I'LL BE GONE, AND YOU'LL HAVE SCORES OF MEN SURROUNDING YOU ON ALL SIDES ASKING FOR YOUR HAND...
WELL...
HE WASN'T ENTIRELY WRONG...

WHAT IS THE NEWS, KOHEN GADOL?
WHAT OF BETHULIA?
IS HOLOFERNES COMING?
MY CHILDREN...
I'VE JUST RECEIVED WORD THAT THE ASSYRIANS SURROUNDING BETHULIA HAVE CUT OFF THE CITY'S WATER SUPPLY.
LET US PRAY FOR THE CITIZENS OF BETHULIA, THAT GOD MAY GIVE THEM THE STRENGTH THEY NEED TO OVERCOME HOLOFERNES.
WHAT IF THEY'RE NOT STRONG ENOUGH, KOHEN GADOL?
WILL GOD SEND THE MESSIAH?

I DON'T KNOW, CHILD.
BUT I KNOW THAT GOD IS WITH US...
AND HE WILL PROTECT HIS CHOSEN PEOPLE... ONE WAY OR ANOTHER.

NO SWEAT...
THAT'S NOT A
GOOD SIGN.

AT LEAST IT WILL
ALL BE OVER IN
FIVE DAYS –
REGARDLESS OF
THE OUTCOME.

THAT IS, UNLESS JUDITH CONVINCED THE ELDERS OTHERWISE... MAYBE I SHOULD STOP BY AND SEE HOW THE MEETING WENT—
UGH... NOW WHICH ONE OF THESE IS HER HOUSE AGAIN?
EXCUSE ME, DO YOU KNOW WHERE JUDITH LIVES?
OH YOU'RE THE NEWCOMER, AREN'T YOU? IT IS SHAMEFUL, BUT WE HAVE NOTHING TO OFFER IN THE WAY OF SUSTENANCE.

CAN I AT LEAST OFFER YOU A PLACE TO GET OUT OF THE SUN FOR A WHILE?
OH, YES. JUDITH. SHE'S QUITE BEAUTIFUL ISN'T SHE? I'M AFRAID YOU'RE TOO LATE THOUGH.
THAT'S ALRIGHT. IF YOU COULD JUST POINT ME IN THE DIRECTION OF JUDITH'S RESIDENCE-
WHAT?
AFTER HER HUSBAND DIED, POOR DEAR, SHE CONSECRATED HERSELF TO OUR LORD.

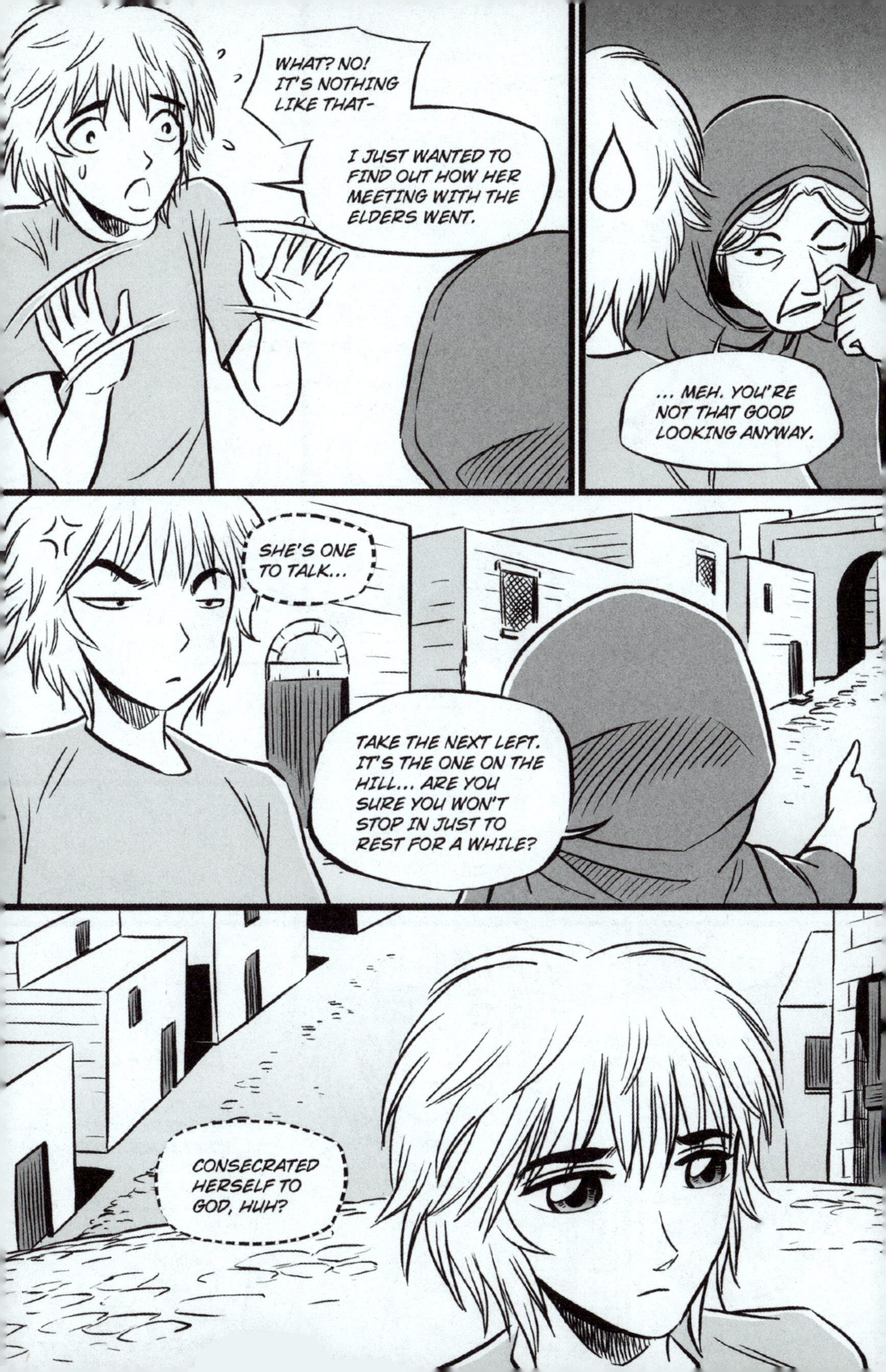

WHAT? NO! IT'S NOTHING LIKE THAT—
I JUST WANTED TO FIND OUT HOW HER MEETING WITH THE ELDERS WENT.
... MEH. YOU'RE NOT THAT GOOD LOOKING ANYWAY.
SHE'S ONE TO TALK...
TAKE THE NEXT LEFT. IT'S THE ONE ON THE HILL... ARE YOU SURE YOU WON'T STOP IN JUST TO REST FOR A WHILE?
CONSECRATED HERSELF TO GOD, HUH?

THAT WOULD EXPLAIN WHY SHE WOULD RATHER STARVE TO DEATH THAN GIVE UP THE TEMPLE.
ALSO MAKES ME LOOK KIND OF WEAK IN COMPARISON.
I THOUGHT I WAS DOING WHAT WAS BEST FOR MY PEOPLE, AND HERE JUDITH IS DOING THE EXACT OPPOSITE...
WHY IS SHE SO DEVOTED?... AND WHAT DOES THAT MAKE ME?

OH WELL. WHAT'S DONE IS DONE AND WHAT WILL BE WILL BE. IT'S NOT LIKE I HAVE A SAY IN THE MATTER ANYWAY.
I'VE DONE ALL I REALLY CAN AGAINST HOLOFERNES... NOW IT'S UP TO THESE PEOPLE.
NOW WHICH HILL WAS IT ON? WAS I SUPPOSED TO TAKE A LEFT UP HERE... OR A RIGHT?

WHUMP
ANOTHER
MESSAGE FROM
NEBUCHADNEZZAR,
MY LORD.

WHAT DOES IT SAY?
THE SAME. HE WANTS YOU TO FOREGO BETHULIA AND CONQUER JERUSALEM.
HMM. NOW SEE, THAT'S A PROBLEM. BECAUSE I WANT TO STAY HERE. AND WE CAN'T BOTH GET WHAT WE WANT NOW CAN WE?
YOUR ORDERS SIR?
"THE SAME."
SO... YOU WILL NOT LEAVE TO TAKE JERUSALEM...

I WILL DO NO SUCH THING.

ARE YOU SURE THIS IS WISE, MY LORD? BETHULIA IS, AFTER ALL, DEPENDENT ON JERUSALEM.

I WILL NOT GIVE UP UNTIL I HAVE IT.

I WILL NOT BE BEATEN. I WILL NOT MOVE ON.

AND I WILL BE TAKING NO MORE ORDERS.

HERE.
BRING ME
SOMETHING
TO DRINK.
WHAT WOULD
YOU LIKE MY
LORD?
MORE, BAGOAS...
MUCH MORE.

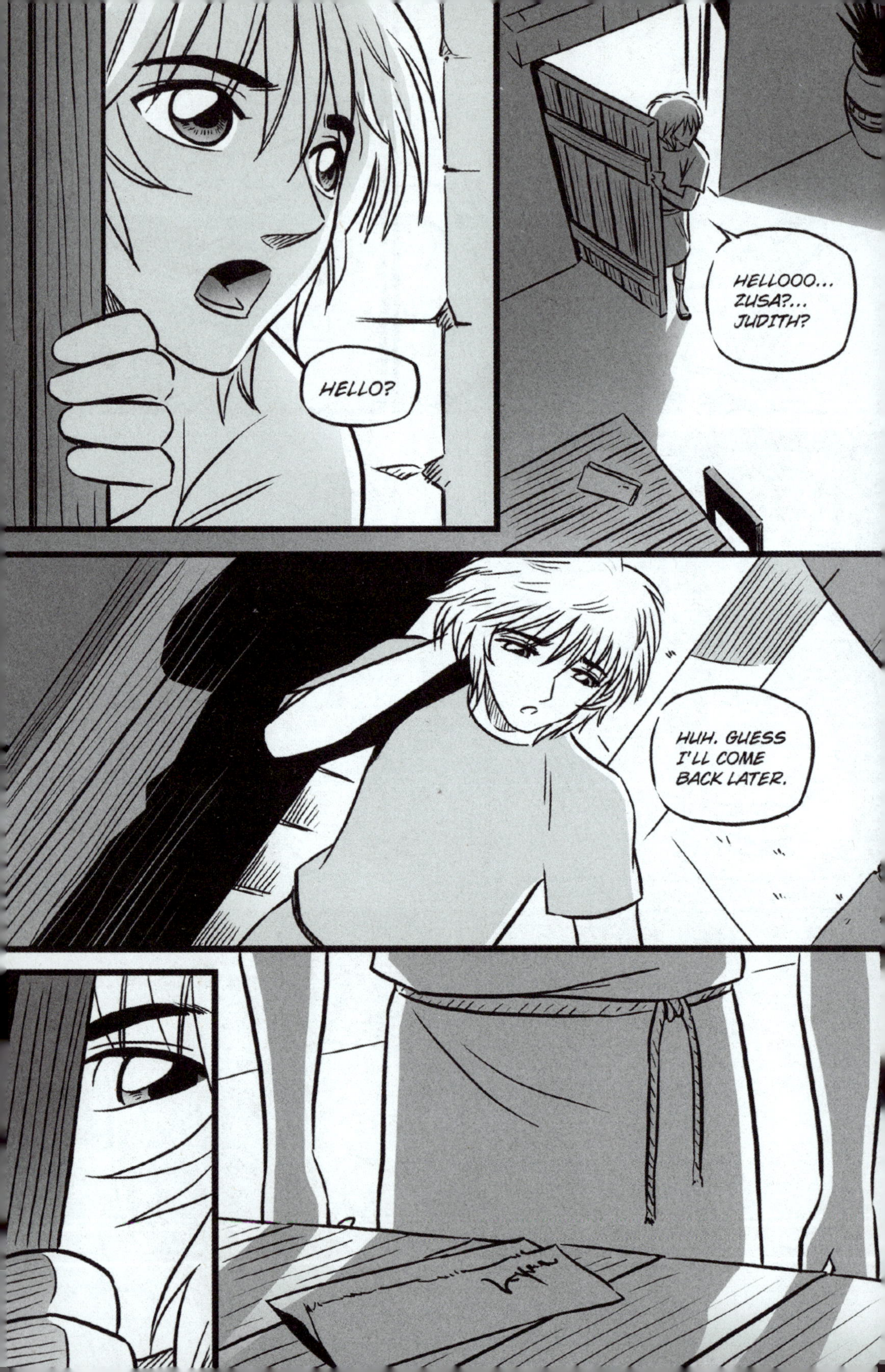

HELLOOO... ZUSA?... JUDITH?
HELLO?
HUH. GUESS I'LL COME BACK LATER.

YOU'VE GOT TO SEE THIS! REGIMENT SIX JUST CAPTURED A JEWISH WOMAN!
WHAT'S SHE LOOK LIKE?
YOU HAVE TO SEE HER FOR YOURSELF! THEY'RE BRINGING HER TO MEET HOLOFERNES!
HEY, DID YOU HEAR?
THE REGIMENT ON PATROL JUST RETURNED. THEY BROUGHT A JEWISH WOMAN WITH THEM!
HAVE YOU SEEN HER YET?
NO, THEY'RE TAKING HER TO THE LIEUTENANT RIGHT NOW!
GET OUT OF BED AND COME SEE!

WHISPER
MY LORD...
FINALLY...
BRING HER HERE.

WHAT DO I DO
WHAT DO I DO
WHAT DO I DO...
ALRIGHT, CALM DOWN. I'M THE LEADER OF AN ENTIRE PEOPLE - ER, WAS. LET'S LOOK AT THIS LOGICALLY.
THERE'S NO WAY THEY WOULD GET THEMSELVES INTO THAT KIND OF TROUBLE. ESPECIALLY AFTER JUDITH'S NEGOTIATION WITH THE ELDERS LAST NIGHT.
THIS IS PROBABLY WHAT THEY PLANNED TO DO BEFORE JUDITH TALKED TO THE ELDERS... THEY PROBABLY ALL WORKED TOGETHER AND FOUND A COMPROMISE.

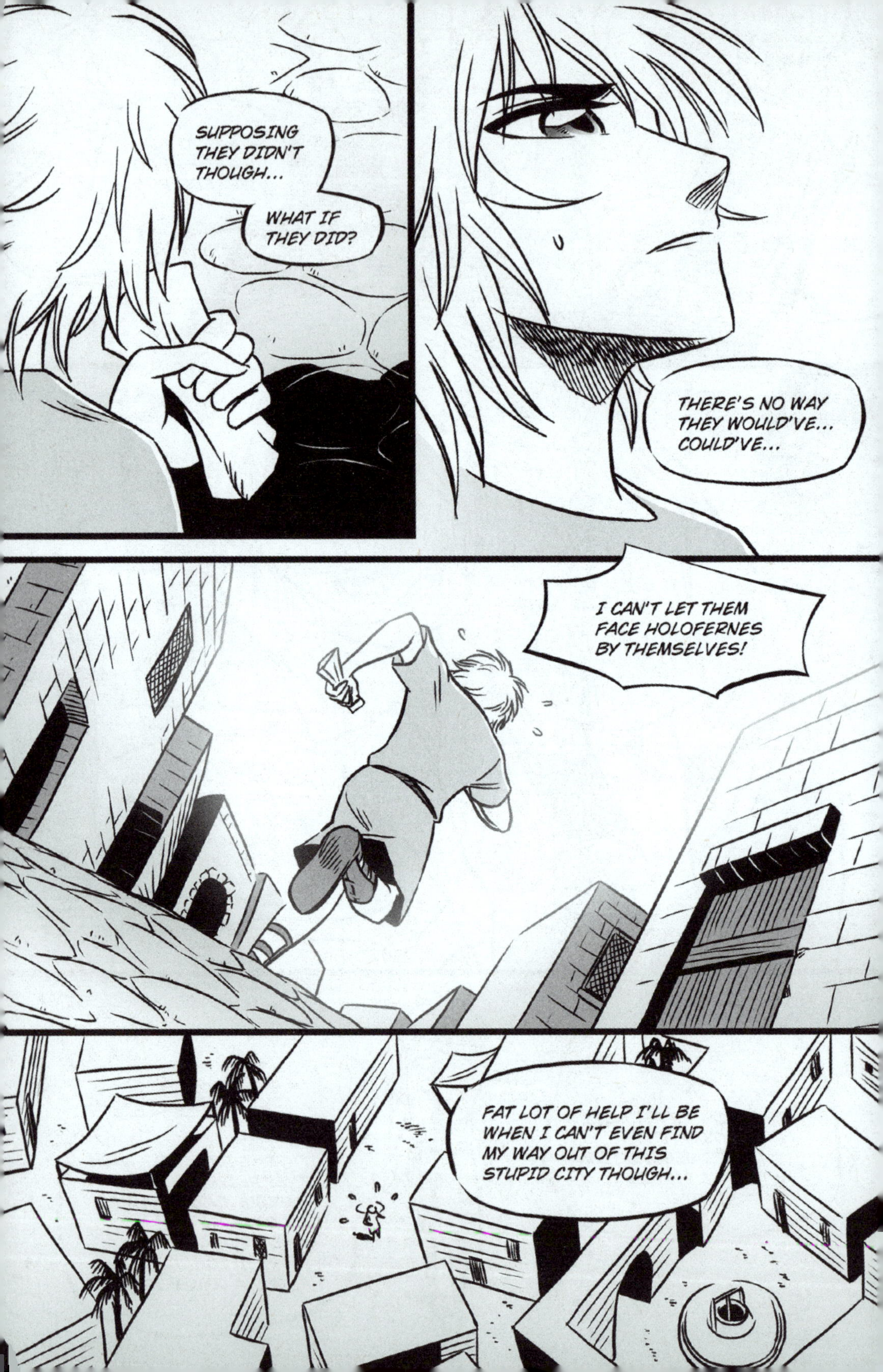

SUPPOSING THEY DIDN'T THOUGH...
WHAT IF THEY DID?
THERE'S NO WAY THEY WOULD'VE... COULD'VE...
I CAN'T LET THEM FACE HOLOFERNES BY THEMSELVES!
FAT LOT OF HELP I'LL BE WHEN I CAN'T EVEN FIND MY WAY OUT OF THIS STUPID CITY THOUGH...

WOAH! YOU WEREN'T KIDDING!
CAN YOU SEE HER?
SHE'S GORGEOUS!
ARE YOU SCARED?
UM...
THE LORD WILL PROTECT US, ZUSA.
... JUST REMEMBER WHY WE'RE DOING THIS... AND STICK TO THE PLAN.

RIGHT. THE PLAN. JUDITH, WE DIDN'T EVEN BRING A WEAPON—
STEP ASIDE! ALL OF YOU!
THIS WOMAN IS HOLOFERNES' HONORED GUEST. UNTIL HOLOFERNES HAS PASSED JUDGMENT YOU MAY NOT TOUCH HER.

HOLOFERNES HAS BEEN TOLD OF YOUR ARRIVAL AND INTENTIONS...
FOLLOW ME.
THIS SHOULD BE MOST INTERESTING...

OPEN THE GATES!
WHAT IS THAT GUY THINKING?
THUNK
HURRY AND OPEN THEM! PLEASE!
OPEN THE GATES!

AREN'T YOU PEOPLE LISTENING?
DID THEY COME THROUGH HERE? HAVE YOU SEEN THEM?
CALM DOWN, SIR. WHAT SEEMS TO BE THE-
WHO SIR?
TWO WOMEN - JUDITH AND ZUSA - DID THEY COME THROUGH HERE?
WE ARE UNDER STRICT ORDERS NOT TO OPEN THIS GATE.
BUT DID YOU SEE THEM?

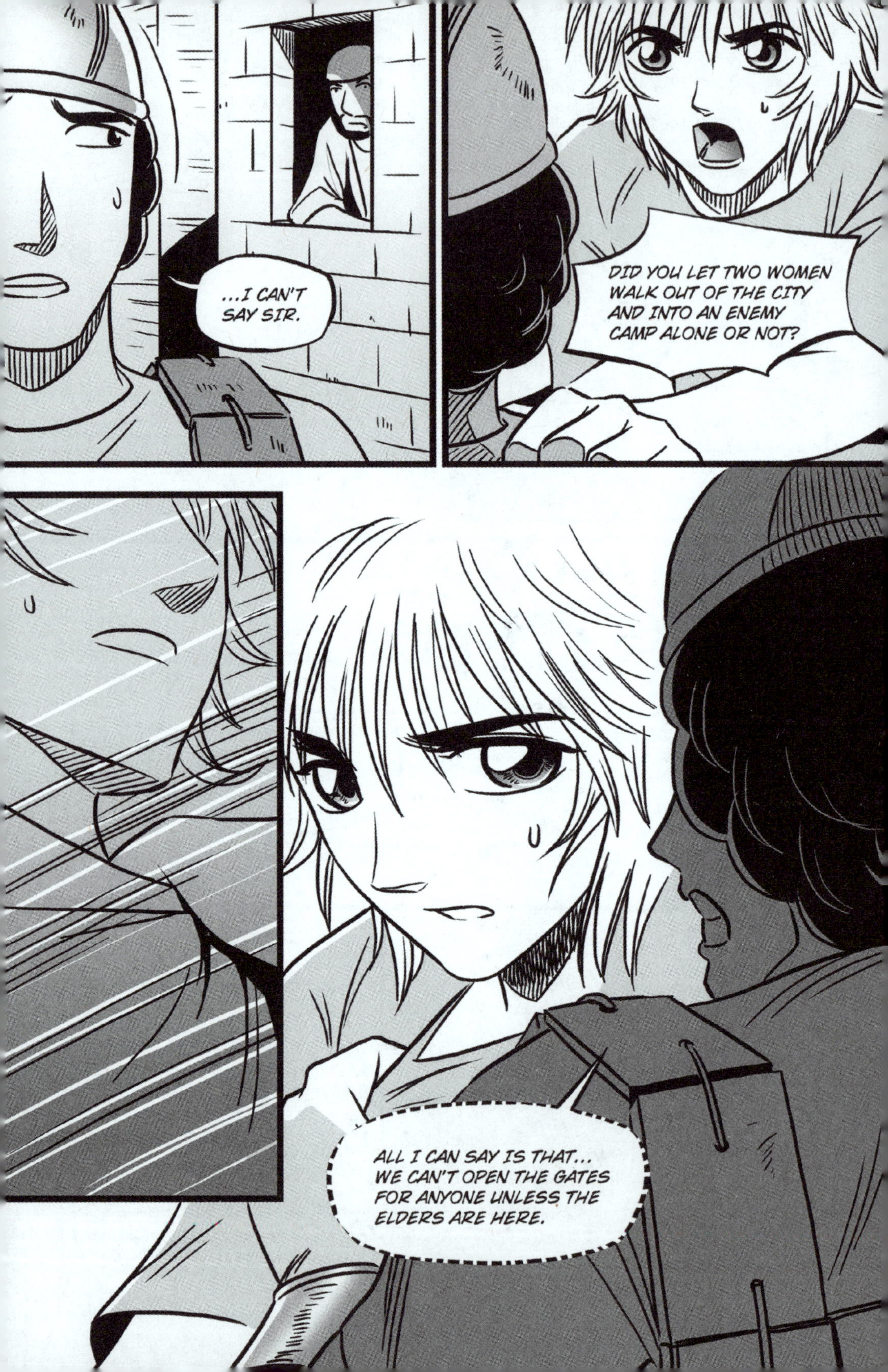
...I CAN'T SAY SIR.
DID YOU LET TWO WOMEN WALK OUT OF THE CITY AND INTO AN ENEMY CAMP ALONE OR NOT?
ALL I CAN SAY IS THAT... WE CAN'T OPEN THE GATES FOR ANYONE UNLESS THE ELDERS ARE HERE.

WAIT HERE.
I DIDN'T HEAR A PLEASE.
WHAT DO YOU MAKE OF HER?
WOULD SHE FIT IN WITH THE OTHERS?
... NO, MY LORD.
PITY... SEND HER IN!

RIGHT THIS WAY, MY LADY.
READY?

MY LORD.

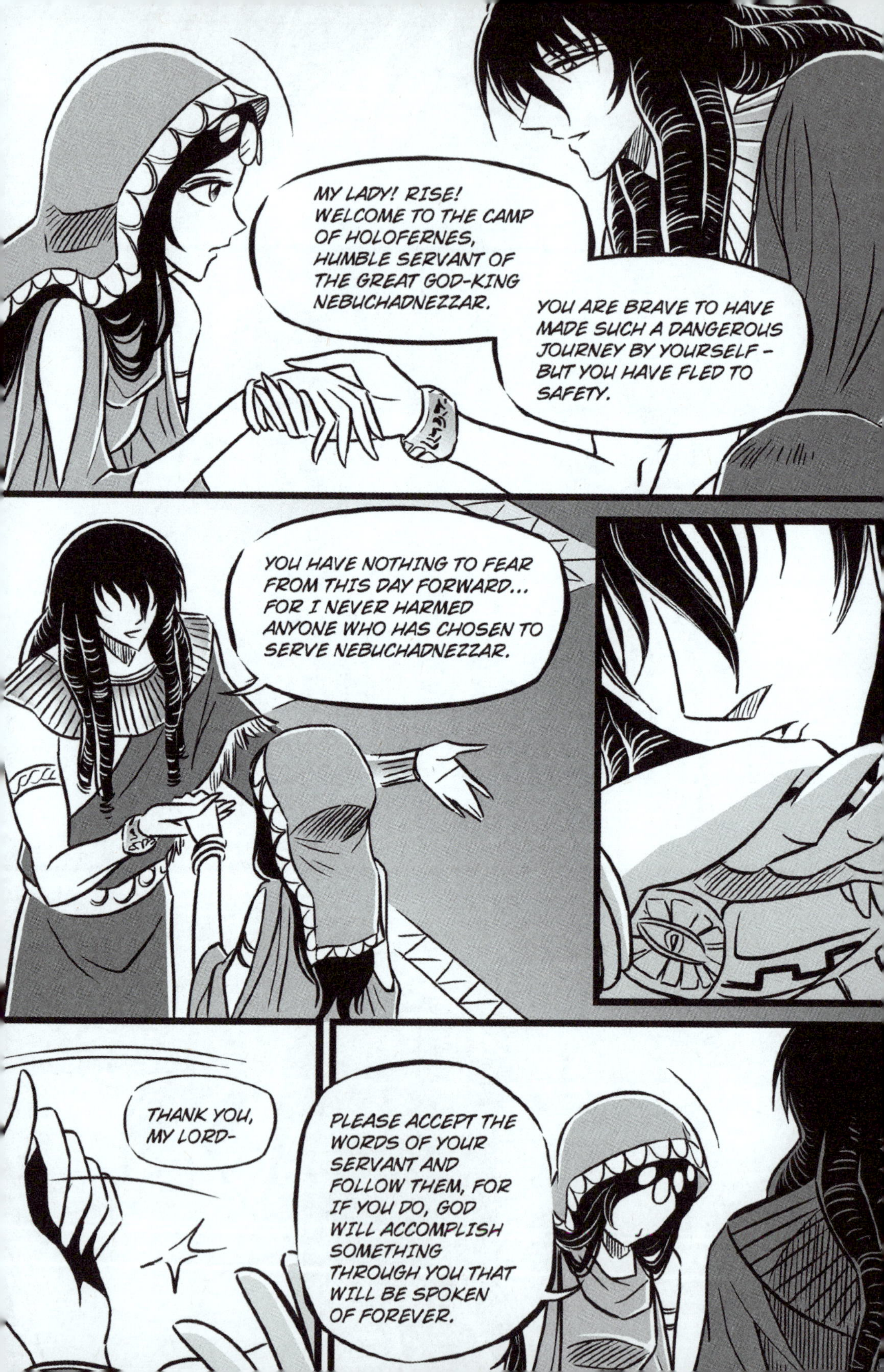

MY LADY! RISE! WELCOME TO THE CAMP OF HOLOFERNES, HUMBLE SERVANT OF THE GREAT GOD-KING NEBUCHADNEZZAR.

YOU ARE BRAVE TO HAVE MADE SUCH A DANGEROUS JOURNEY BY YOURSELF – BUT YOU HAVE FLED TO SAFETY.

YOU HAVE NOTHING TO FEAR FROM THIS DAY FORWARD... FOR I NEVER HARMED ANYONE WHO HAS CHOSEN TO SERVE NEBUCHADNEZZAR.

THANK YOU, MY LORD–

PLEASE ACCEPT THE WORDS OF YOUR SERVANT AND FOLLOW THEM, FOR IF YOU DO, GOD WILL ACCOMPLISH SOMETHING THROUGH YOU THAT WILL BE SPOKEN OF FOREVER.

IS THAT SO?
WORD OF YOUR GREATNESS HAS SPREAD THROUGHOUT THE WHOLE WORLD. EVEN THE ISRAELITES SPEAK HIGHLY OF YOU.
OH YES. WE HAVE HEARD OF YOUR WISDOM AND SKILL IN BATTLE, WHICH IS WHY I KNOW WE CANNOT BEAT YOU.
BUT THEY ALSO SAY YOU ARE THE ONE GOOD MAN IN THE WHOLE ASSYRIAN KINGDOM—
—WHICH IS WHY I KNEW I COULD COME TO YOU.

YOU SAID YOU HAVE COME TO AID MY CAMPAIGN AGAINST BETHULIA - HOW IS IT YOU PLAN ON DOING THAT?
THE MAN YOU LEFT WITH US - ACHIOR OF THE AMMONITES - RECALLED THAT WHICH HE TOLD YOU IN YOUR WAR COUNCIL.
AND WHAT DO YOU MAKE OF HIM?
HE IS A FOOL FOR NOT ACCEPTING YOUR GENEROSITY AND LEADERSHIP-
BUT WHAT HE SAID CONCERNING US WAS TRUE.

WE CANNOT BE PREVAILED UPON UNLESS WE SIN AGAINST OUR GOD.
REALLY? AND WHAT DOES THAT MEAN FOR MY CAMPAIGN?
FORTUNATELY FOR YOU, THE PEOPLE ARE ABOUT TO PROVOKE THEIR GOD TO ANGER.
THEIR FOOD SUPPLY IS EXHAUSTED, SO THEY HAVE PLANNED TO KILL AND EAT ALL THAT GOD HAS FORBIDDEN.
WHAT DO YOU MEAN?

THEY PLAN TO EAT WHAT THEY CONSECRATED FOR THE PRIESTS' USE IN JERUSALEM. BY OUR GOD'S DECREE, WE ARE NOT EVEN ALLOWED TO TOUCH IT.
WHEN I LEARNED OF THIS, I FLED FROM THEM... PLEASE BELIEVE THE WORDS OF YOUR SERVANT.
YOUR DEDICATION TO YOUR CAUSE IS PROOF ENOUGH. OF COURSE I DO.
THAT IS WHERE I AM OF SERVICE TO YOU, MY LORD.
MY ONLY CONCERN IS HOW WE ARE TO KNOW WHEN THEY'VE COMMITTED THIS CRIME?

IN RETURN FOR MY STEADFAST DEVOTION, MY GOD SPEAKS TO ME IN VISIONS. WITH YOUR CONSENT, I WILL GO OUT INTO THE VALLEY TO PRAY EVERY NIGHT, AND HE WILL TELL ME WHEN YOU SHOULD STRIKE.
FOR HE HAS SENT ME TO ACCOMPLISH THINGS THAT WILL ASTONISH THE WHOLE WORLD.
SO BE IT.
TONIGHT... WE WILL HOLD A BANQUET IN HONOR OF THE WOMAN WHO WOULD RISK EVERYTHING TO AID ASSYRIA IN ITS CONQUEST OF JERUSALEM!

WHAT IS YOUR NAME, MY LADY?

JUDITH. DAUGHTER OF MERARI.

JUDITH...

WHAT DO YOU MEAN THEY'RE GONE??
SHE LEFT THE CITY LAST NIGHT—
WHY WOULD THEY DO THAT? WHAT COULD SHE POSSIBLY HOPE TO ACCOMPLISH??
SHE DIDN'T SAY.

AND YOU JUST LET THEM WALK OUT?
WHAT ELSE COULD WE DO?
WHERE ARE YOU GOING?
AFTER THEM.

AND YOU'RE GOING TO OPEN THE GATE FOR ME.
NO!
GET OUT OF MY WAY!
ALL YOU WOULD DO IS ENDANGER THEIR MISSION.
I DON'T THINK THEY COULD BE ANY MORE ENDANGERED THAN THEY ALREADY ARE.

WHATEVER THEY HAVE PLANNED MIGHT BE JEOPARDIZED IF YOU ARE RECOGNIZED.
SO WE'RE STUCK IN HERE...
WHILE EVERYONE'S LAST HOPE IS OUT IN THE MIDDLE OF THE ASSYRIAN CAMP... PERFECT.

TONIGHT WE HONOR JUDITH...
-THROUGH WHOSE INTERCESSION, THE ASSYRIANS WILL CONQUER THE ENTIRE EARTH!
YOU HAVE MY THANKS MY LADY.

AND MY SOLEMN OATH, THAT I WILL PROTECT YOU FROM ALL HARM FROM THIS DAY FORWARD.
...THANK YOU, MY LORD.
YOU'RE SO TENSE, MY DOVE! YOU MUST BE EXHAUSTED FROM YOUR JOURNEY. YOU SHOULD RELAX...
BAGOAS! BRING OUR HONORED GUEST SOME OF MY BEST WINE.
OH, NO THANK YOU MY LORD, I—
AH! I WON'T TAKE NO FOR AN ANSWER!
ASSYRIAN VINEYARDS ARE SOME OF THE BEST! SOMEONE AS ELEGANT AS YOURSELF WILL APPRECIATE IT.

AND AFTER ALL...
EVEN FLOWERS NEED WATER.
NO, THANK YOU...
MY LADY WILL ONLY TAKE FROM WHAT SUPPLIES SHE HAS COME WITH.
MY! BUT IT'S ONLY SOME GRAIN! A DELICATE FLOWER SUCH AS YOURSELF SHOULD BE FEASTING MORE LAVISHLY, DON'T YOU AGREE?

NO THANK YOU, MY LORD... I CANNOT EAT YOUR FOOD, UNLESS I WANT TO ANGER GOD TOO.
BUT WHAT IF YOUR SUPPLY RUNS OUT? WHERE CAN WE GET MORE LIKE IT FOR YOU?
YOUR SERVANT WILL NOT USE UP THESE THINGS BEFORE THE LORD CARRIES OUT BY MY HAND WHAT HE HAS DETERMINED TO DO.
...I SEE...
AS YOU WISH, MY DOVE.

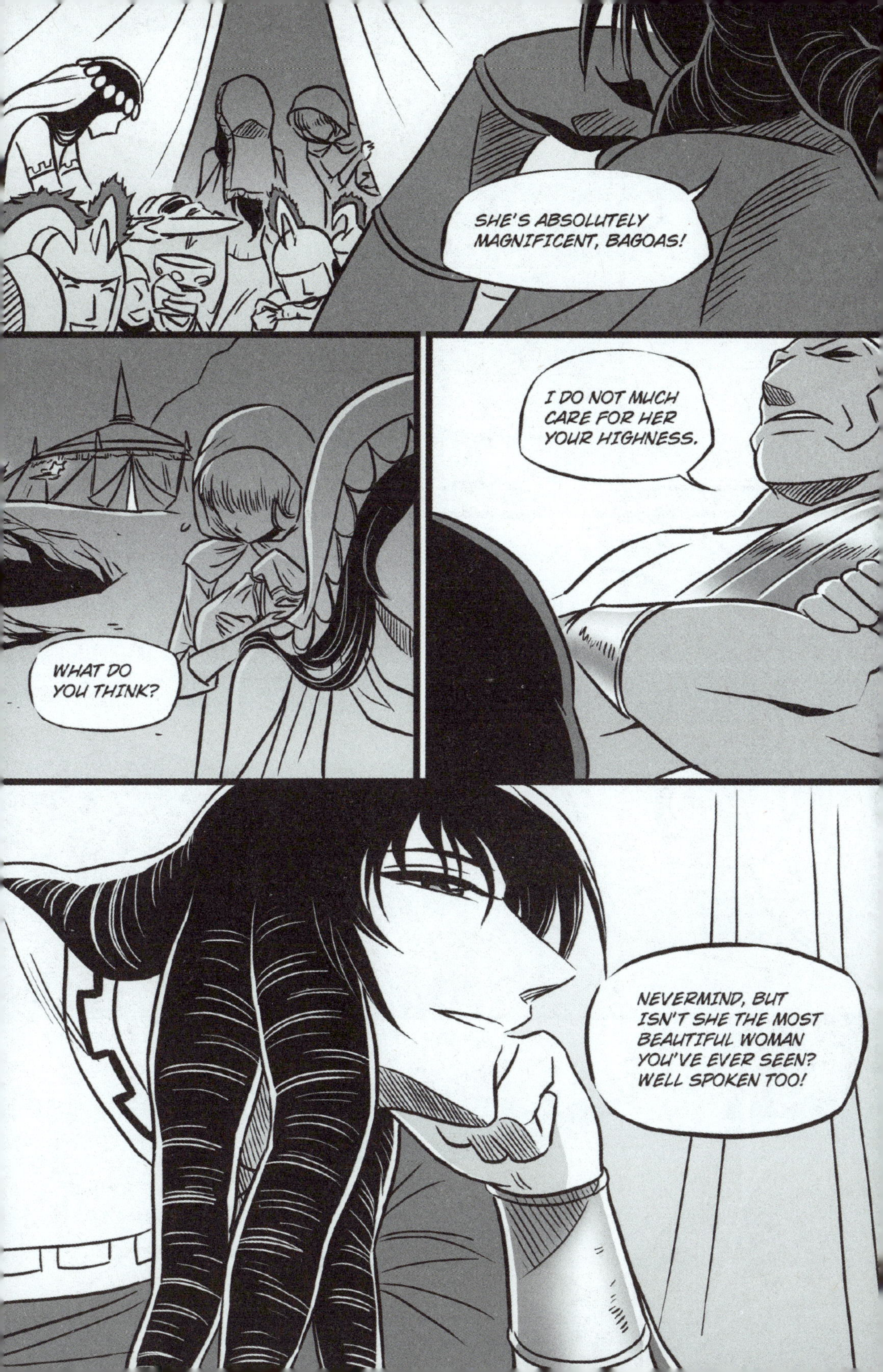

SHE'S ABSOLUTELY MAGNIFICENT, BAGOAS!
WHAT DO YOU THINK?
I DO NOT MUCH CARE FOR HER YOUR HIGHNESS.
NEVERMIND, BUT ISN'T SHE THE MOST BEAUTIFUL WOMAN YOU'VE EVER SEEN? WELL SPOKEN TOO!

THE WAY SHE CARRIES HERSELF... IT'S LIKE SHE'S NOT SCARED OF ANYTHING.
AND SOMETHING ABOUT HER...
SHE HAS A STRENGTH - A DRIVE... A POWER.
I WANT IT.

MY LORD?
SHE WON'T BE EASY TO WIN OVER.
THE USUAL TACTICS DIDN'T SEEM TO WORK AT DINNER TONIGHT—
IF I MAY, MY LORD?
I THINK YOU SHOULD HAVE NOTHING TO DO WITH HER.
WHATEVER DO YOU MEAN?
SHE'S A FAIR MATCH.
YOU SAY THAT LIKE IT'S A BAD THING.

THAT IS...
I THINK YOU'VE MET YOUR MATCH IN HER.
LEAVE ME.
...
I WANT IT.

GOOD MORNING,
BEAUTIFUL.

HOW DID
YOU SLEEP?

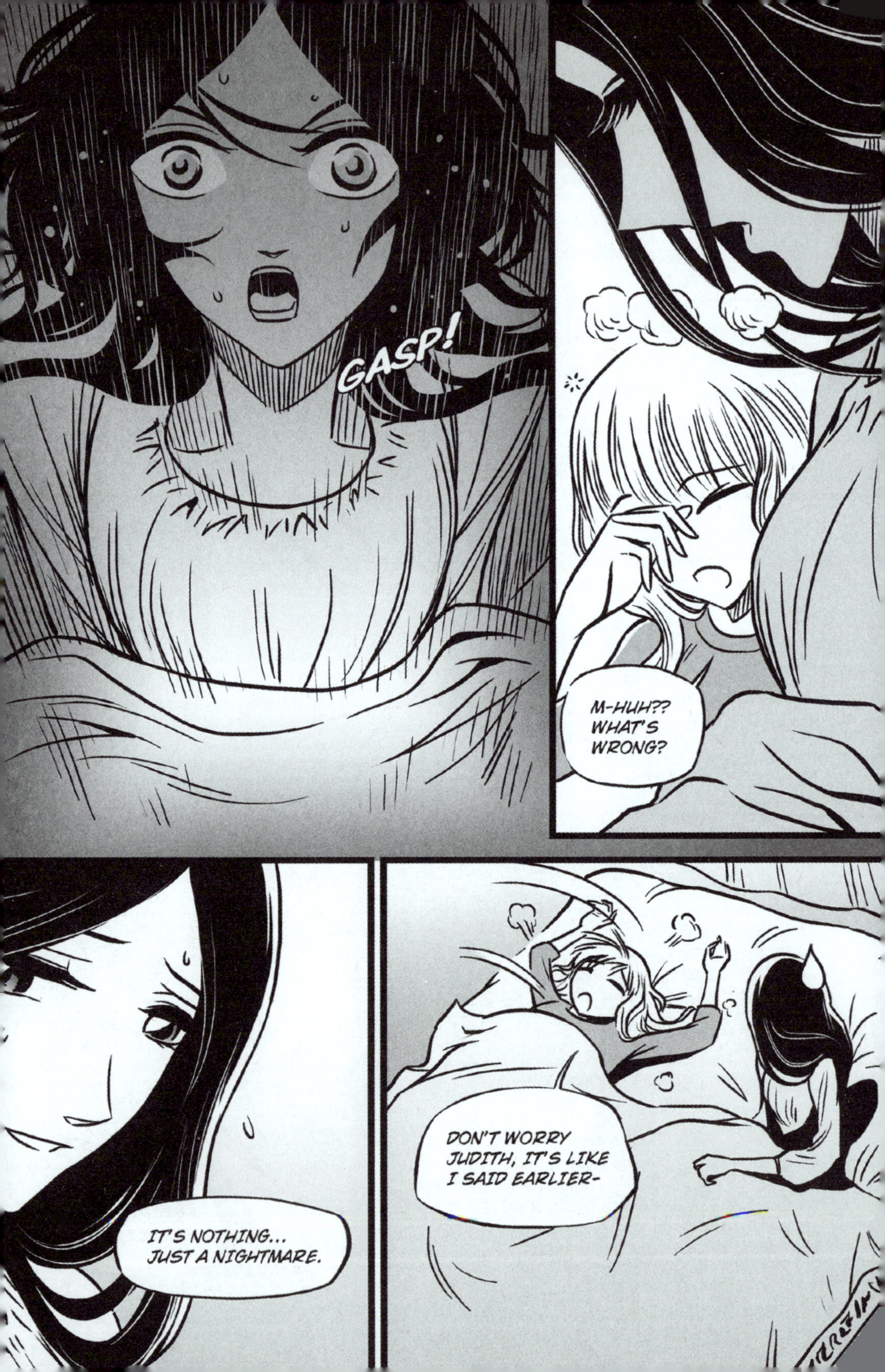

GASP!
M-HUH?? WHAT'S WRONG?
IT'S NOTHING... JUST A NIGHTMARE.
DON'T WORRY JUDITH, IT'S LIKE I SAID EARLIER-

YOU CAN TAKE HIM...
SO WHAT DO YOU THINK OF HOLOFERNES?
HE SEEMS LIKE HE'LL BE REALLY EASY TO FOOL.
... I'M NOT SO SURE.

I'M NOT SURE YET... BUT HE COULDN'T BE THIS SUCCESSFUL IN HIS CAMPAIGN IF HE WERE REALLY AS INFANTILE AS HE ACTED TONIGHT.
WHAT DO YOU MEAN?
HE'S SECOND IN COMMAND OVER ALL ASSYRIA – A MILITARY GENIUS. I THINK THIS IS ALL STRATEGY –
YOU THINK HE'S ACTING THE PART?
WELL WHAT ABOUT YOU?
HE'S CLEVER...

HUH?
THE FACT THAT YOU MADE A PLAN AND HAD THE NEXT FOUR DAYS MAPPED OUT THIS MORNING PROVES YOU'RE MORE THAN A MATCH FOR HIM.
I CERTAINLY HOPE I'M NOT A MATCH FOR HIM.
YOU KNOW WHAT I MEAN!
IF ANYONE CAN OUTSMART HIM, IT'S YOU.
I HOPE YOU'RE RIGHT, ZUSA...

I JUST HAVE TO REMEMBER WHY I'M DOING THIS...
GOD GIVE ME STRENGTH.

DID YOU SEE THAT WOMAN LAST NIGHT?
TALK ABOUT LUCKY! HOLOFERNES GETS ALL THE GOOD ONES.
HOW LONG DO YOU THINK BEFORE HE BREAKS HER?
A DAY.
HA! GOOD LUCK WITH THAT WOMAN!
I BET YOU! HE'S GOT QUITE AN IMPRESSIVE RECORD. HE MIGHT HAVE EVEN MORE WOMEN THAN NEBUCHADNEZZAR!
SHE'S ON ANOTHER LEVEL! SHE MIGHT BE THE FIRST ONE THAT GOT AWAY.
WELL NONE OF US HAVE A CHANCE, THAT'S FOR SURE.
HE CAN PULL IT OFF. HOLOFERNES IS A GOOD LOOKIN' GUY - AND A SMOOTH TALKER!

HA! HE CAN HAVE HER!
OH, COME ON. DON'T TELL ME YOU'RE NOT JEALOUS!
NO WAY! THAT WOMAN SCARES ME!
JUST BY THE LOOKS OF HER I KNOW SHE'S OUT OF MY LEAGUE! SHE MUST BE A NOBLE OR SOMETHING AMONG HER PEOPLE.
NAH, THEY SAY SHE'S AN ORDINARY CITIZEN.
SERIOUSLY? MAKES YOU THINK... WHAT THE REST OF THE WOMEN MUST BE LIKE.
YOU IDIOT. STOP AND THINK ABOUT THE OTHER HALF OF THE POPULATION.
THEIR MEN ARE GOING TO BE MORE THAN A MATCH FOR US.
JUST IMAGINE... A LINE OF THEIR ELITE WARRIORS ASSEMBLED OUTSIDE THEIR GATES... MARCHING STACCATO DIRECTLY TOWARD US.
OOF, I HOPE I NEVER LIVE TO SEE THAT DAY!

DAY TWO.
UGH! THIS IS TORTURE!
YEAH. MAYBE I MISSED SOMETHING THE FIRST HUNDRED TIMES I READ IT...

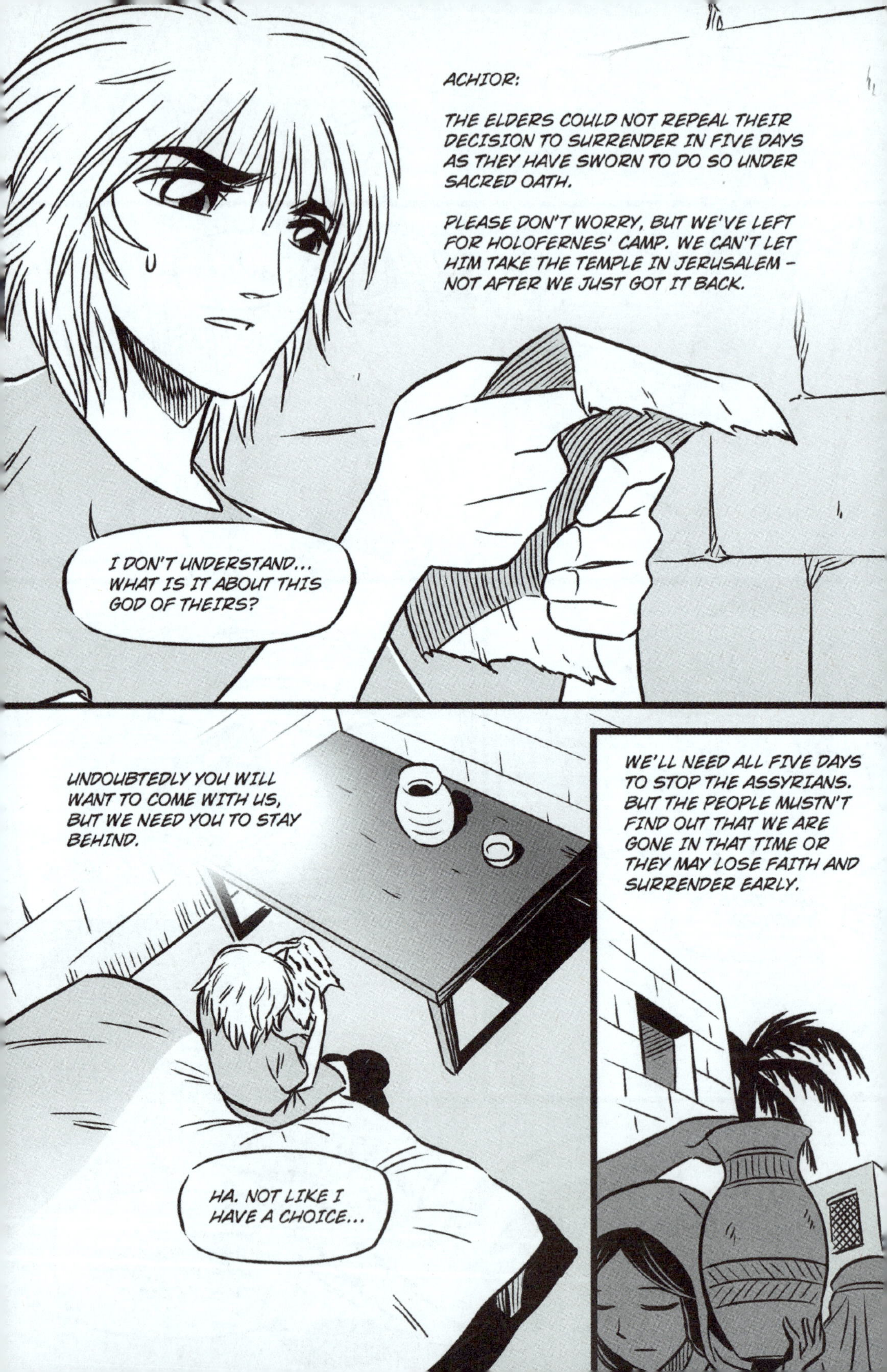

ACHIOR:

THE ELDERS COULD NOT REPEAL THEIR DECISION TO SURRENDER IN FIVE DAYS AS THEY HAVE SWORN TO DO SO UNDER SACRED OATH.

PLEASE DON'T WORRY, BUT WE'VE LEFT FOR HOLOFERNES' CAMP. WE CAN'T LET HIM TAKE THE TEMPLE IN JERUSALEM – NOT AFTER WE JUST GOT IT BACK.

I DON'T UNDERSTAND... WHAT IS IT ABOUT THIS GOD OF THEIRS?

UNDOUBTEDLY YOU WILL WANT TO COME WITH US, BUT WE NEED YOU TO STAY BEHIND.

HA. NOT LIKE I HAVE A CHOICE...

WE'LL NEED ALL FIVE DAYS TO STOP THE ASSYRIANS. BUT THE PEOPLE MUSTN'T FIND OUT THAT WE ARE GONE IN THAT TIME OR THEY MAY LOSE FAITH AND SURRENDER EARLY.

IT WILL BE UP TO YOU TO MAKE SURE THAT OUR ABSENCE REMAINS SECRET. I'M COUNTING ON YOU.
SURE. LAY THE GUILT TRIP ON ME. NO PROBLEM.
I MEAN, WHY NOT? YOU'RE OUT FACING THE CONQUEROR OF WORLDS, AND I'M STUCK KEEPING IT HUSH-HUSH.
I MEAN... MY JOB KINDA PALES IN COMPARISON...
DID YOU HEAR? JUDITH'S MISSING!
WHAT?
DID THE ASSYRIANS CAPTURE HER?
PEOPLE OVERHEARD THE GATEKEEPERS SAY SHE LEFT TWO NIGHTS AGO!

I WISH TO APOLOGIZE TO YOU, MY LADY.
WHY EVER WOULD YOU DO THAT, MY LORD?

YOU HAVE GONE THROUGH SO MUCH IN THE PAST FEW DAYS BECAUSE OF ME – I CAN'T IMAGINE HOW HARD IT MUST HAVE BEEN FOR YOU TO LEAVE YOUR OWN PEOPLE.
I FEEL ABSOLUTELY TERRIBLE – IF ONLY THEY HAD NOT SLIGHTED ME, NONE OF THIS WOULD'VE HAPPENED!
PLEASE DON'T WORRY YOURSELF. AFTER ALL, THEY BROUGHT THIS ON THEMSELVES.
THERE IS NO ONE YOU NEED TO WORRY ABOUT, MY LORD – ZUSA IS ALL I HAVE.
I APPRECIATE YOUR WILLINGNESS TO FORGIVE, BUT I WILL NOT PARDON MYSELF SO EASILY. I HAVE CAUSED YOU IMMENSE GRIEF, I AM SURE, BY WARRING ON YOUR KITH AND KIN.

WHAT ABOUT YOUR HUSBAND?

WHAT DOES HE THINK ABOUT ALL THIS?

MY HUSBAND PASSED AWAY THREE YEARS AGO-

I HAVE SERVED MY GOD EVER SINCE.
OH... MY POOR DOVE...
I CAN'T IMAGINE WHAT YOU ARE GOING THROUGH.

IT'S NOTHING, MY LORD—
NO.
IT'S MUCH MORE THAN NOTHING. YOU'VE GIVEN UP EVERYTHING, AND DONE SO MUCH FOR US...
I HOPE I CAN SOMEHOW RETURN THE FAVOR...

EXCUSE ME.
I THINK IT IS TIME WE WENT OUT TO PRAY.
...OF COURSE.
UNTIL TOMORROW, MY DOVE.

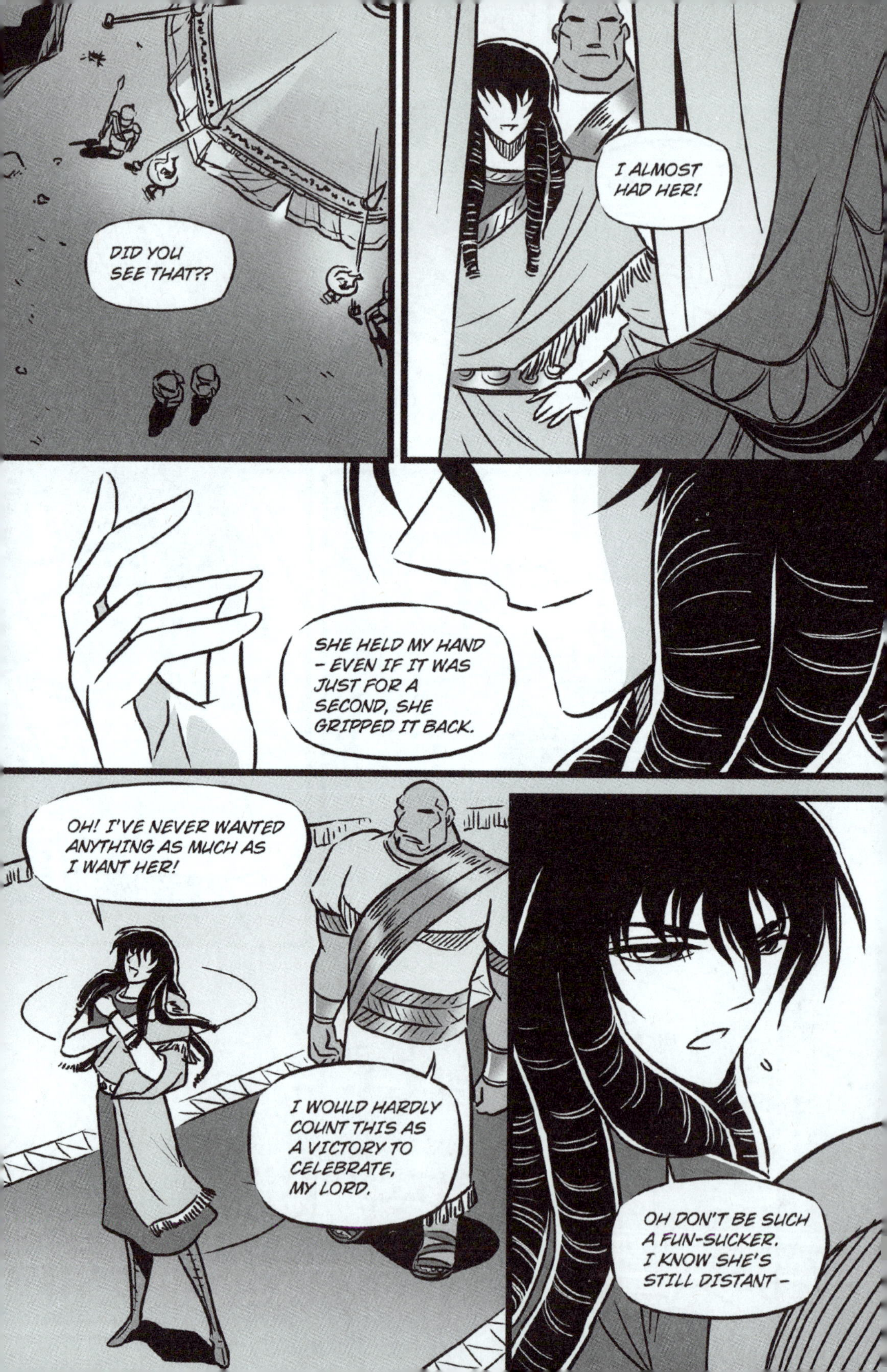

DID YOU SEE THAT??
I ALMOST HAD HER!
SHE HELD MY HAND — EVEN IF IT WAS JUST FOR A SECOND, SHE GRIPPED IT BACK.
OH! I'VE NEVER WANTED ANYTHING AS MUCH AS I WANT HER!
I WOULD HARDLY COUNT THIS AS A VICTORY TO CELEBRATE, MY LORD.
OH DON'T BE SUCH A FUN-SUCKER. I KNOW SHE'S STILL DISTANT —

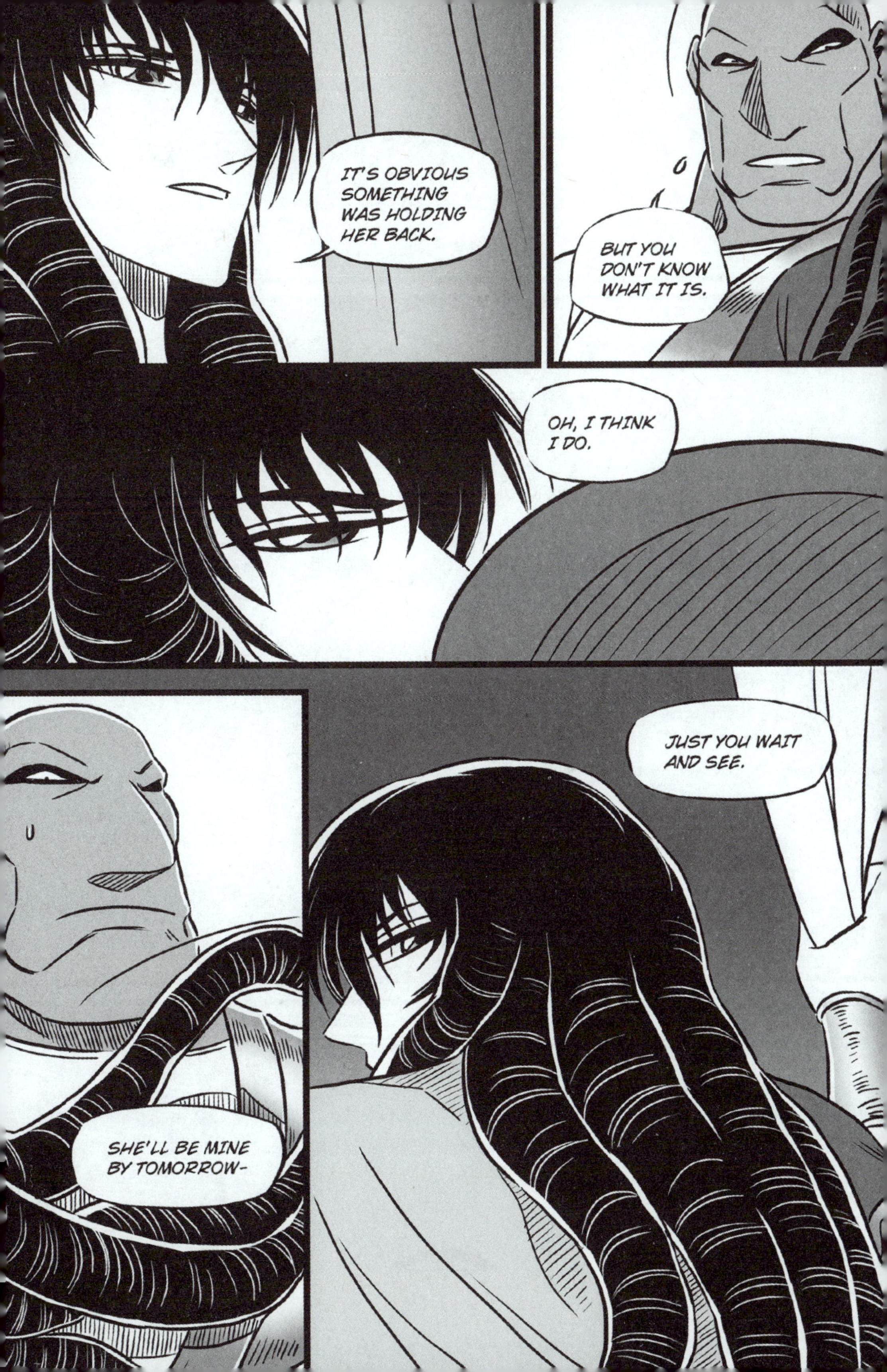

IT'S OBVIOUS SOMETHING WAS HOLDING HER BACK.
BUT YOU DON'T KNOW WHAT IT IS.
OH, I THINK I DO.
JUST YOU WAIT AND SEE.
SHE'LL BE MINE BY TOMORROW-

"WHAT ABOUT YOUR HUSBAND?"
WHAT DOES HE THINK ABOUT ALL THIS?
WHAT DOES HE THINK?...

MANASSEH!
I'VE MISSED YOU SO MUCH!
GASP

... MANASSEH?
MANASSEH?...
WHAT'S WRONG...?
WHY, JUDITH?
I'M... DOING
THIS FOR GOD!
AND OUR PEOPLE!
WHY?

YOU TOLD ME TO! ON YOUR DEATH BED! YOU TOLD ME TO DO MY PART!
WHY –
STOP IT MANASSEH! I'M DOING THIS FOR YOU!
ARE YOU?
WHAT DO YOU... WHAT DO YOU MEAN?
HAVE YOU FORGOTTEN ME ALREADY?

NO! NEVER! I'LL NEVER FORGET!
I'M DOING THIS FOR YOU!
OH JUDITH...
DON'T WORRY MY DOVE.
I HOPE TO RETURN THE FAVOR...

THIS DEFINITELY WASN'T IN THE JOB DESCRIPTION.
WHERE'S JUDITH?
SHE WAS CLOSER TO GOD THAN ANY OF US! IF SHE LEFT, WHAT HOPE DO WE HAVE?
NOW CALM DOWN, YOU DON'T KNOW FOR SURE WHETHER SHE ACTUALLY LEFT OR NOT.
DON'T EVEN TRY TO PULL THAT ONE! WE ALL OVERHEARD YOU THE OTHER MORNING.

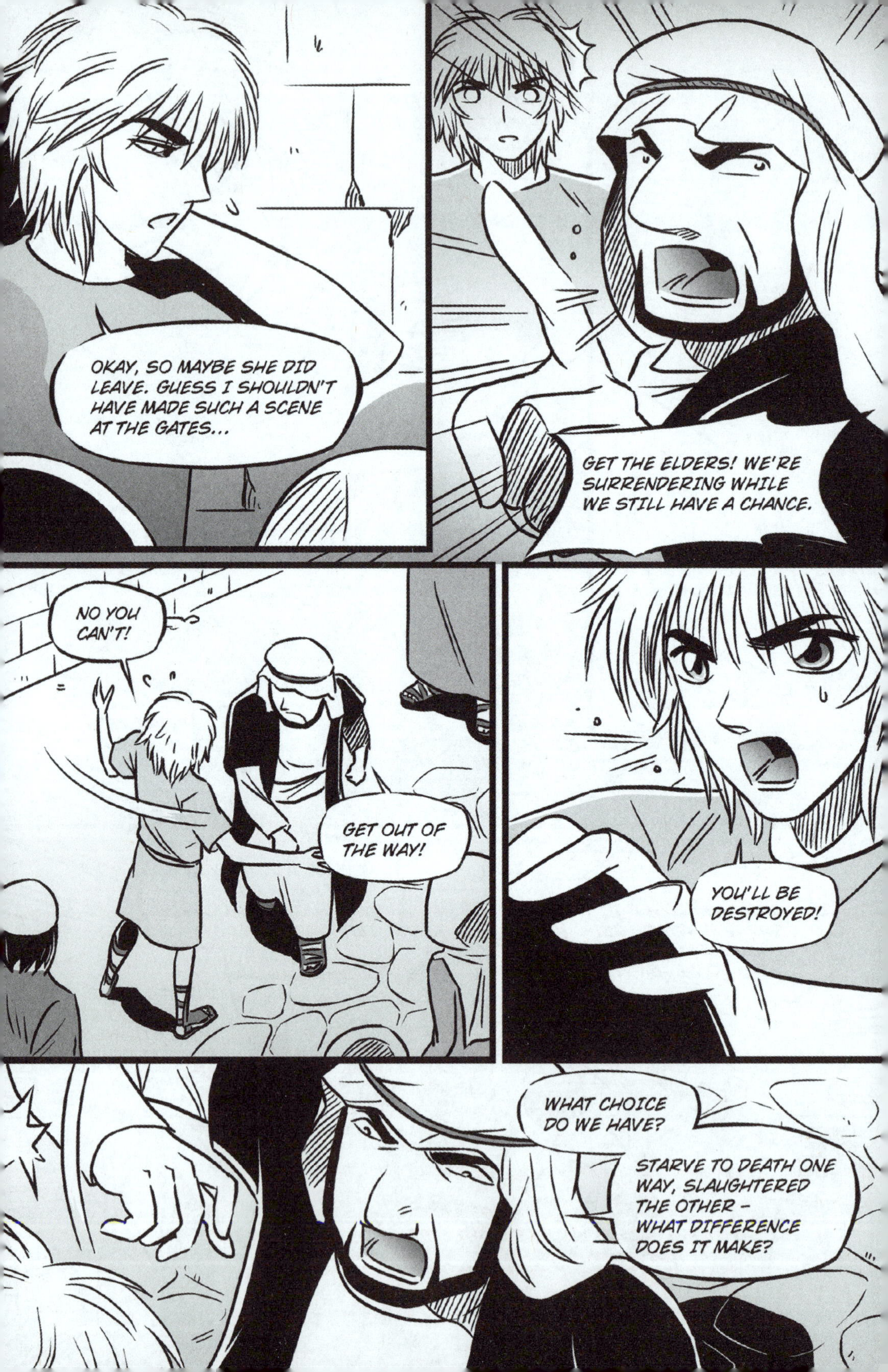

OKAY, SO MAYBE SHE DID LEAVE. GUESS I SHOULDN'T HAVE MADE SUCH A SCENE AT THE GATES...
GET THE ELDERS! WE'RE SURRENDERING WHILE WE STILL HAVE A CHANCE.
NO YOU CAN'T!
GET OUT OF THE WAY!
YOU'LL BE DESTROYED!
WHAT CHOICE DO WE HAVE?
STARVE TO DEATH ONE WAY, SLAUGHTERED THE OTHER – WHAT DIFFERENCE DOES IT MAKE?

ALL THE DIFFERENCE!
JUDITH IS RISKING HER LIFE FOR YOU AND YOUR GOD.
WHY SHOULD WE BELIEVE YOU? YOU'RE JUST AN AMMONITE. YOU DON'T EVEN BELIEVE IN GOD.
BUT I BELIEVE IN THEM... AND I'M 'JUST AN AMMONITE.'
...FINE.

WE'LL WAIT ONE MORE DAY.
BUT ON THE FIFTH DAY - THOSE GATES ARE OPENING.
THEY BETTER MAKE IT BACK SAFELY, YOU HEAR?
HE SURE BETTER EXIST AFTER ALL THIS...

LORD HOLOFERNES? WHAT'S WRONG?
YOU'RE NOT YOURSELF LATELY!
I FEEL A DRAFT.
ARE YOU ALRIGHT?

THE NIGHTS ARE GROWING COLDER.
YES.
ANY NEWS? OR MUST YOU BRAVE THE WEATHER TO PRAY AGAIN TONIGHT?
I AM SORRY, MY LORD. HE HAS NOT SAID ANYTHING YET.
EXPLAIN TO ME SOMETHING, JUDITH.
YES, MY LORD?

HOW CAN YOU TRUST SOMEONE WHO TOOK YOUR HUSBAND AWAY?
... IT IS NOT MY PLACE TO QUESTION GOD'S WILL.
SUCH FAITH-FULNESS IN A WOMAN... IF ONLY THE ASSYRIANS WERE MORE LIKE YOU.
MY LORD, YOU EXALT ME TOO HIGHLY.
YOU'RE FAR TOO MODEST... AFTER ALL, IT'S BECAUSE OF YOUR VIRTUE THAT YOU RECEIVE THESE VISIONS, RIGHT?

THE GLORY BELONGS TO GOD... I AM ONLY HIS SERVANT.
I SEE...
JUDITH...
I WANT YOUR GOD... TO BE MY GOD.
..WHAT?

WHY... WHY EVER WOULD YOU WANT THAT, MY LORD?
OH, I SEE...
I THOUGHT BY YOUR DEVOTION THAT HE MIGHT MEAN MORE TO YOU...
OH, NO, HE DOES – IT'S JUST, THE QUESTION WAS SO SUDDEN...
BUT YES, HE MEANS MORE TO ME THAN ANYTHING ELSE...
IF YOUR GOD MEANS THAT MUCH TO YOU, DON'T YOU THINK IT'S IMPORTANT THAT HE MEANS THAT MUCH TO ME AS WELL?
Y... YES, I SUPPOSE-

FOR MY CAMPAIGN DEPENDS ON YOUR GOD'S INTERVENTION.
IF YOUR GOD IS AIDING IN THE DESTRUCTION OF HIS OWN PEOPLE, I CANNOT HOPE THAT HE WILL FIND ANY MORE FAVOR WITH US.
YOU THINK MY INTENTIONS ARE PURELY SELFISH...
SO... YOU WISH TO ENSURE THAT HIS LOYALTIES LIE WITH YOU?
BUT SEEING HOW YOU DUTIFULLY SERVE YOUR GOD FOR ALL HE'S DONE FOR YOU MAKES ME FEEL I OUGHT TO DO THE SAME.
AFTER ALL, IF IT WEREN'T FOR HIM...

I NEVER WOULD'VE MET YOU.
...
JUDITH?...
WILL YOU TEACH ME
YOUR GOD'S WAYS?
..."YOU SHALL LOVE
THE LORD YOUR
GOD ALONE..."

EXCUSE ME...
I THINK IT'S TIME I WENT. PERHAPS GOD WILL SPEAK TO ME TONIGHT.
COME ALONG, ZUSA.

WHY DON'T YOU SPEND ANY TIME WITH US ANYMORE? I'VE BEEN SO BORED LATELY...
WHAT IS IT? WHAT'S WRONG?
SOMETHING'S TROUBLING YOU... I CAN TELL.
YOU HAVEN'T COME IN SO LONG—
IS IT THE JEWESS?
SLAP

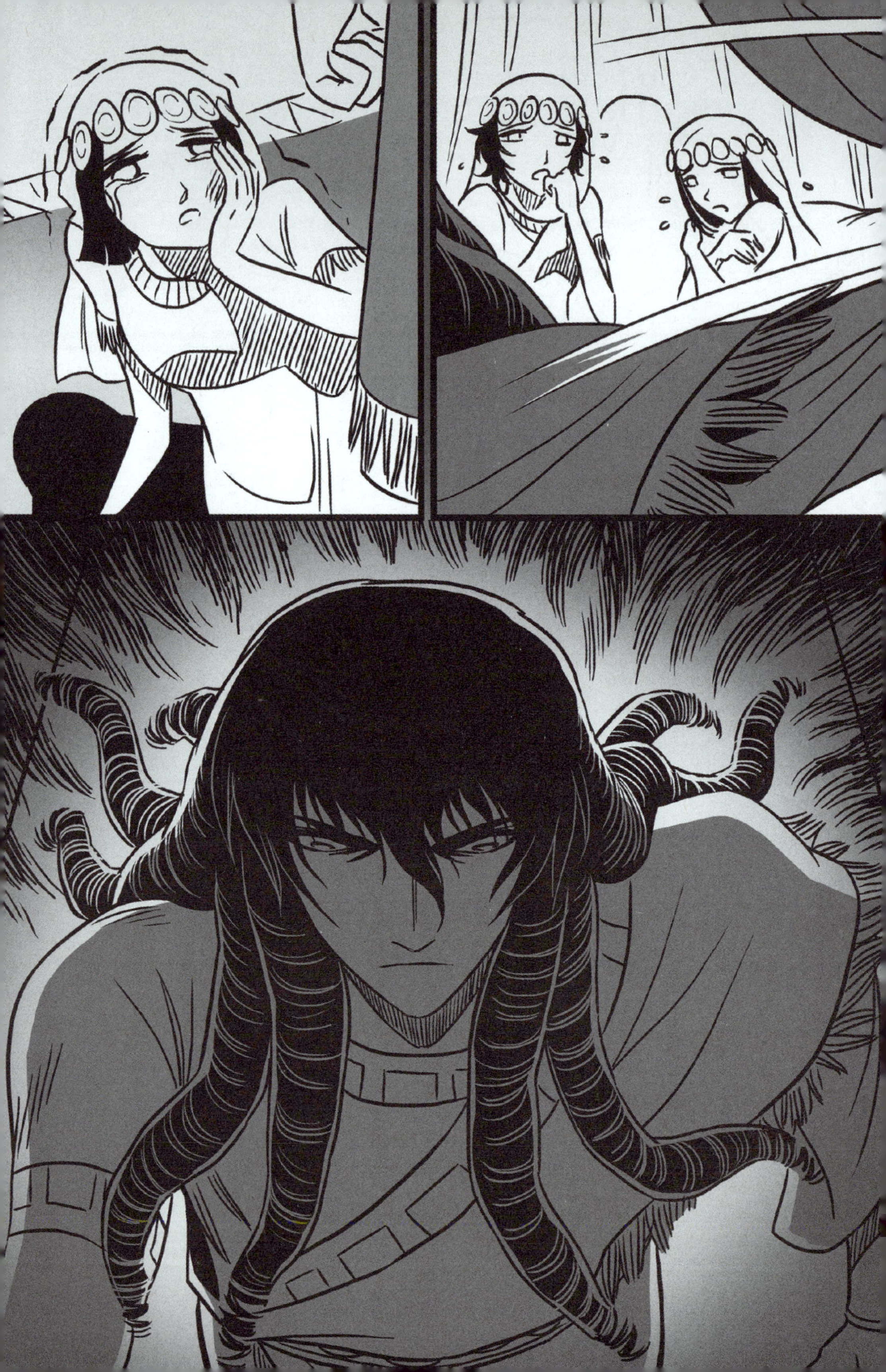

UGH
WHAT'S WRONG JUDITH?
CAN'T SLEEP.
WHY?
WHAT IF I AM DOING THIS FOR MYSELF?
WHAT IF I'M NOT DOING THIS FOR THE REASONS I THINK I AM, ZUSA?
JUDITH, THAT'S INSANE. YOU ARE THE MOST SELFLESS PERSON I KNOW.

AM I?
FOR HEAVEN'S SAKE, JUDITH, WHY DO YOU THINK I'M DOING THIS??
I'M ONLY HERE IN THE MIDDLE OF THIS GOD-FORSAKEN CAMP FOR YOU! AND I WOULDN'T EVEN BE HERE IF YOU WEREN'T!
... ZUSA...
WHEN WE FIRST MET... IT WAS YOU WHO SHOWED ME WHAT IT MEANT TO SERVE OTHERS...

MATCHMAKER PLEASE! ISN'T THERE ANYONE?
YOUR FAMILY IS JUST TOO FAR IN DEBT. THERE ISN'T EVEN A DOWRY TO OFFER.
I'M SORRY, BUT THERE'S NOTHING I CAN DO FOR YOU.

WHAT ARE WE GOING TO DO, MOTHER?
OH I DON'T KNOW!
WE CAN ONLY PAY OFF OUR DEBTS IF WE MARRY YOU TO SOMEONE WEALTHY—
AND THE ONLY WAY WE CAN DO THAT IS BY GIVING THEM MONEY WE DON'T HAVE! HOW SHOULD I KNOW WHAT WE'RE SUPPOSED TO DO?

IT'S TOO BAD YOU AREN'T MORE DESIRABLE...
KNOCK
KNOCK
HELLO, I BROUGHT SOME EXTRA BREAD - SURPLUS FROM MY HUSBAND'S WORK IN THE FIELD.
WHY, JUDITH!
THANK YOU... IT MEANS A LOT TO US.

THESE ARE HARD TIMES FOR US FINANCIALLY.

REALLY? IS THERE ANYTHING I CAN DO TO HELP?

BEFORE I KNEW IT...

I WAS WORKING FOR YOU AND YOUR HUSBAND TO PAY OFF MY MOTHER'S DEBT SO I COULD ACTUALLY HAVE A DOWRY FOR MYSELF.

YOU AGREED TO HELP US OUT OF THE KINDNESS OF YOUR HEART.

I WAS ONLY IN IT FOR MYSELF.

SO STOP BEING SO CRITICAL OF YOURSELF AND GO TO SLEEP.
WHAT WAS I THINKING?? I CAN'T BELIEVE I JUST SAID ALL THAT!

GOOD MORNING BEAUTIFUL...
WHAT IS IT, JUDITH? TELL ME...

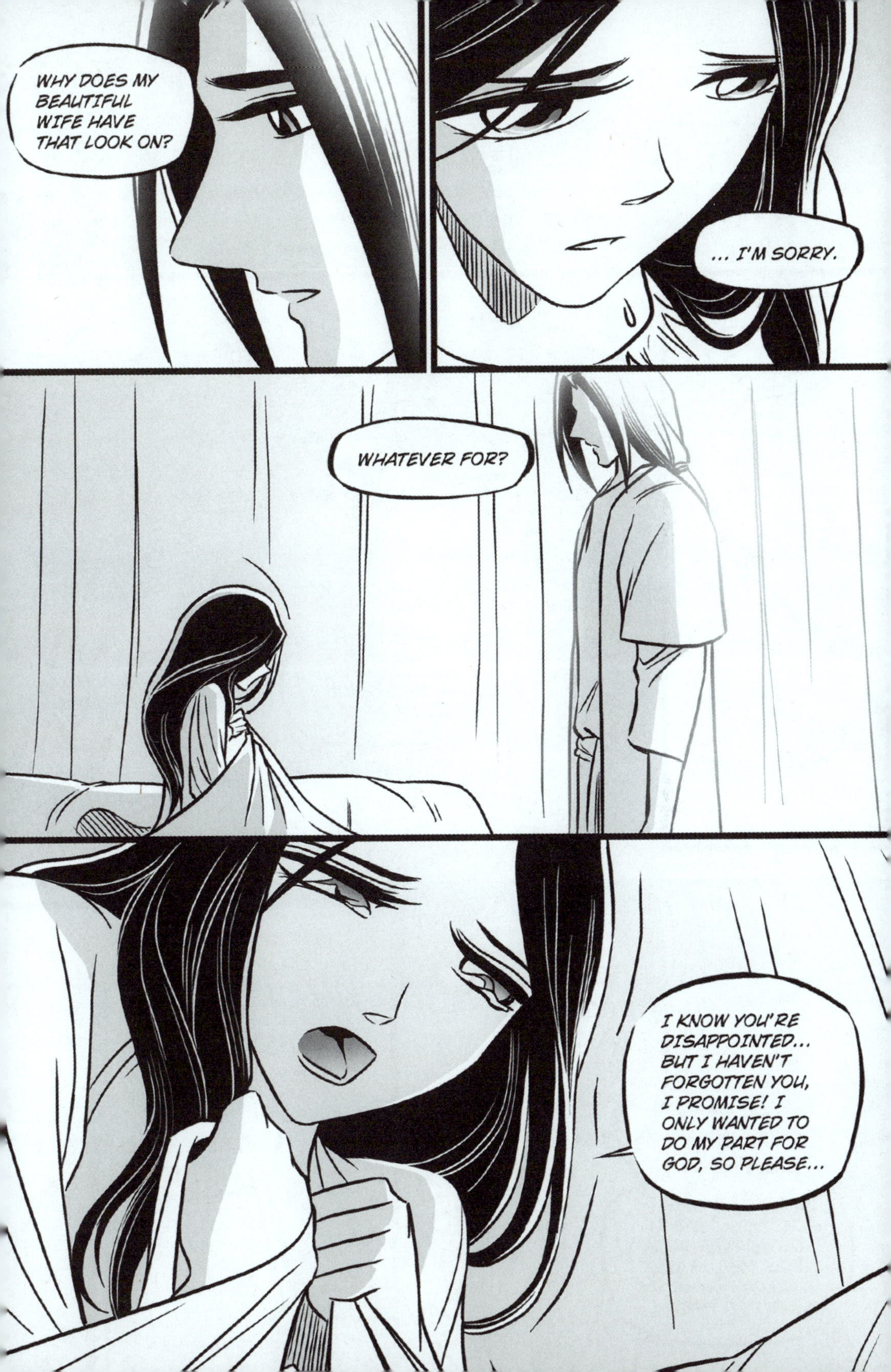

WHY DOES MY BEAUTIFUL WIFE HAVE THAT LOOK ON?

... I'M SORRY.

WHATEVER FOR?

I KNOW YOU'RE DISAPPOINTED... BUT I HAVEN'T FORGOTTEN YOU, I PROMISE! I ONLY WANTED TO DO MY PART FOR GOD, SO PLEASE...

DON'T BE UPSET...
OH JUDITH...
HOW COULD I BE ANYTHING BUT PROUD OF YOU?
BUT LOOK AT THE POSITION I'M IN! HOLOFERNES GROWS MORE AGGRESSIVE EACH DAY - WHAT IF I CAN'T DO THIS?
HA HA HA

JUDITH! YOU'RE TOO HARD ON YOURSELF!
YOU CAN DO IT. WE'LL BE HERE FOR YOU.

READY?
INFORM HOLOFERNES... THAT GOD HAS SPOKEN.
THIS IS IT.
TIME'S UP.
TONIGHT...

A PRIVATE AUDIENCE WILL BE THE PERFECT WAY TO MAKE SURE...
THIS DINNER...
ALL THE EFFORTS OF THE PAST THREE DAYS COME TO FRUITION.
WILL DECIDE EVERYTHING.
IT ALL ENDS TONIGHT.

MY LORD.
JUDITH.
PLEASE... JOIN ME.
TONIGHT WE CELEBRATE OUR IMMINENT VICTORY OVER THE ISRAELITES.

A TOAST?
IF IT PLEASES MY LORD, THEN I WILL CONSENT TO DRINK AND COMMEMORATE THE MAGNITUDE OF THIS DAY.
ZUSA...
OH! JUDITH...
... I CAN'T FIND THE BAG.

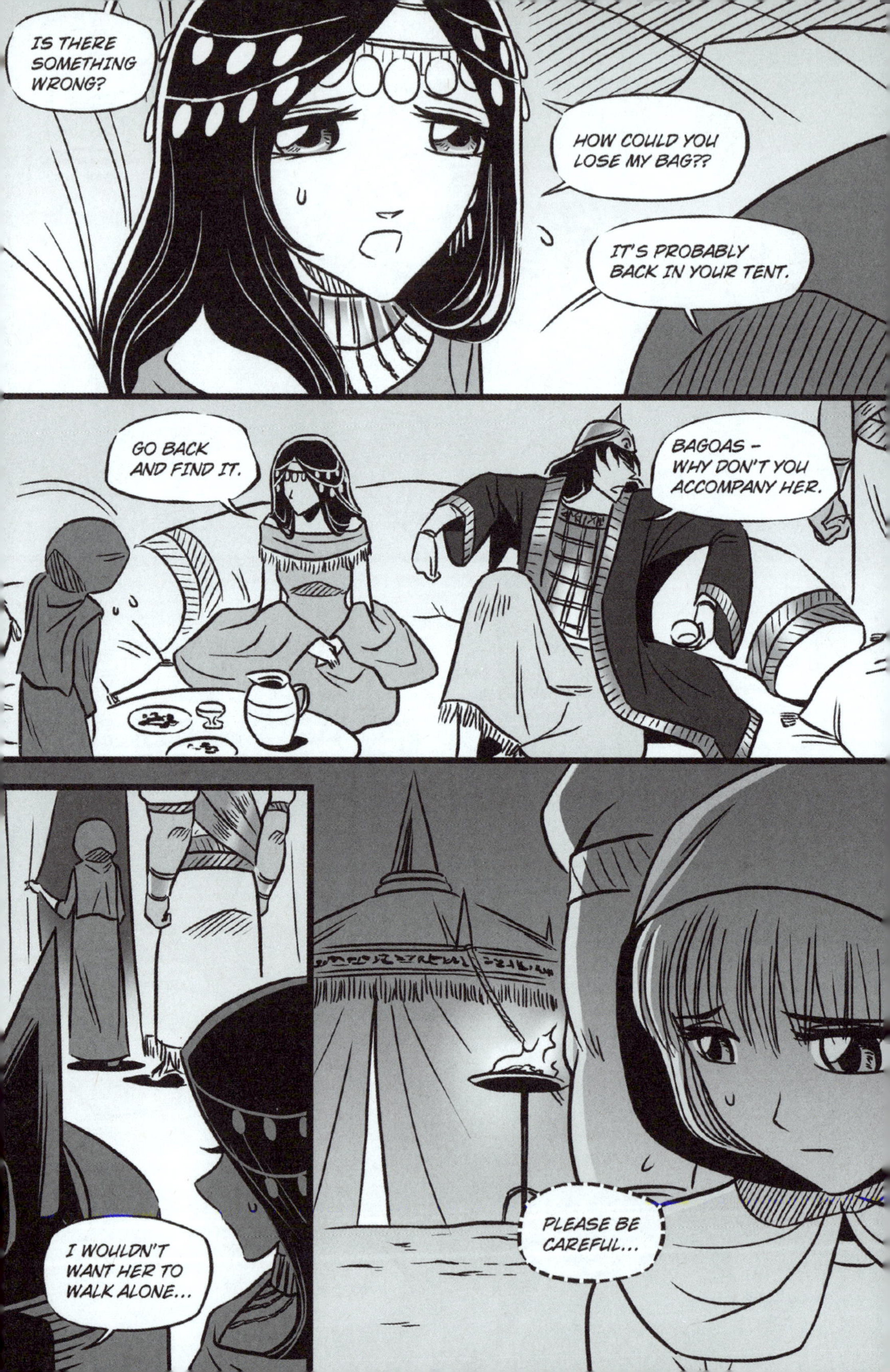

IS THERE SOMETHING WRONG?
HOW COULD YOU LOSE MY BAG??
IT'S PROBABLY BACK IN YOUR TENT.
GO BACK AND FIND IT.
BAGOAS — WHY DON'T YOU ACCOMPANY HER.
I WOULDN'T WANT HER TO WALK ALONE...
PLEASE BE CAREFUL...

CRACKLE
AND...
HOW ARE YOU
THIS EVENING,
MY LORD?...
IS SOMETHING AILING
YOU, MY LORD? YOU SEEM
DIFFERENT TONIGHT.
DO I?
NOT AS WELL AS
I HAVE BEEN OR
WILL BE.

EXQUISITE.
I'VE DENIED MYSELF FOR TOO LONG.
AND YET... THIS DINNER LEAVES SOMETHING TO BE DESIRED.
HERE. QUENCH YOUR THIRST.
WOULD YOU LIKE MORE, MY LORD?

YES. I WILL.
PLEASE, MY LORD, LET ME GO HELP MY MAID –
I WISH YOU WOULDN'T CALL ME THAT.
–MY LORD?

ISN'T IT OBVIOUS? I CONSIDER YOU MUCH MORE THAN A SERVANT...
EXCUSE ME?
IT'S NOT THAT HARD TO UNDERSTAND. I'M ASKING IF YOU WANT TO BE QUEEN OF THE ASSYRIANS.
I WANT YOU BY MY SIDE WHEN I CONQUER THE WORLD.
MY LORD, YOU FORGET YOU ARE THE SERVANT OF NEBUCHADNEZZAR –
WHO DO YOU THINK IS NEXT IN LINE FOR THE THRONE?

WEALTH... POWER... IT'S ALL YOURS.
IF YOU JUST... BECOME MINE...
NO! MY LORD, I MUST REFUSE. I—
DON'T REJECT ME!

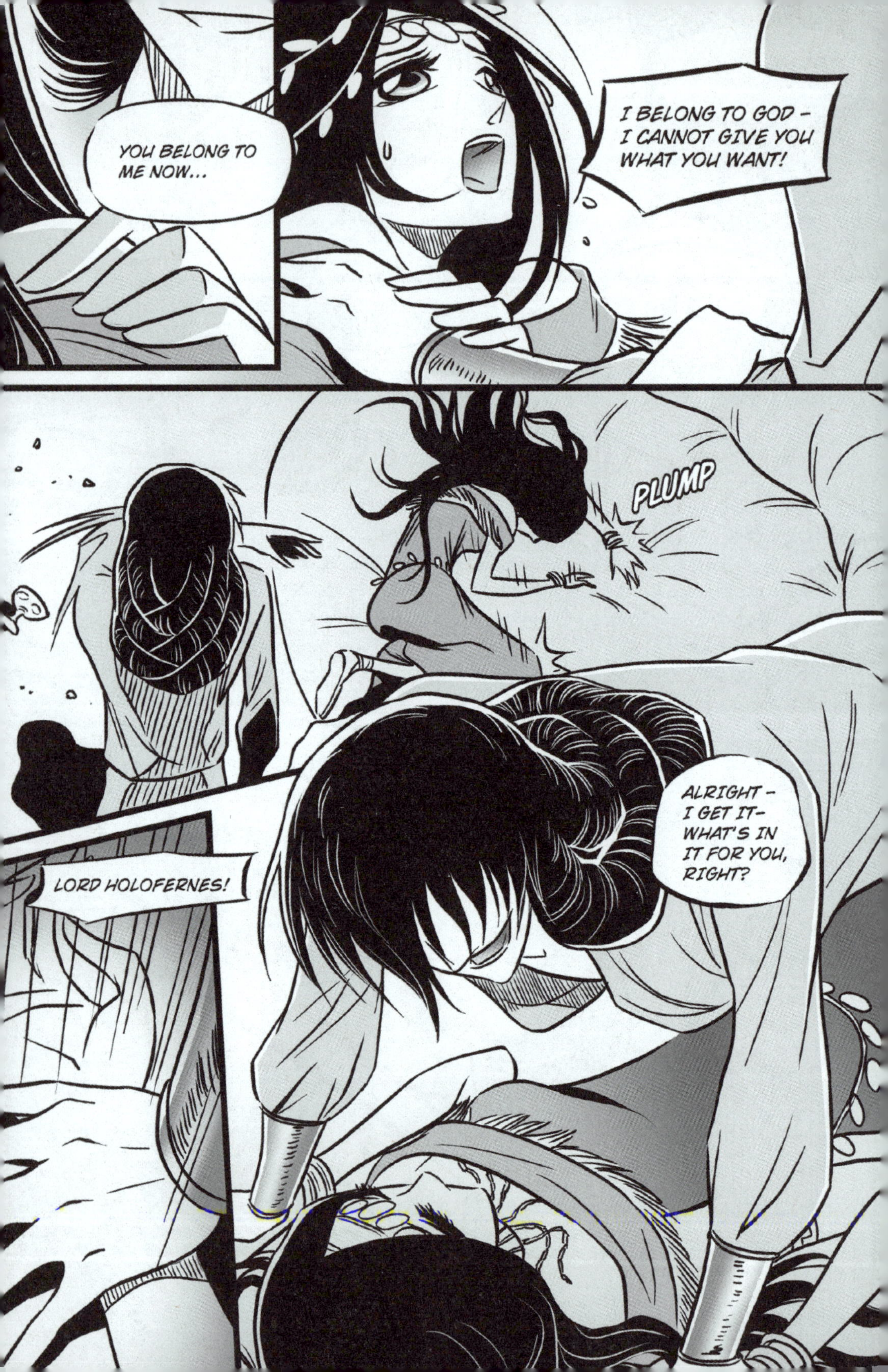
YOU BELONG TO ME NOW...
I BELONG TO GOD — I CANNOT GIVE YOU WHAT YOU WANT!
PLUMP
LORD HOLOFERNES!
ALRIGHT — I GET IT— WHAT'S IN IT FOR YOU, RIGHT?

NAME YOUR PRICE. WHATEVER YOU WANT. IT'S YOURS.
PLEASE! I DON'T WANT ANYTHING!
YOU KNOW, PLAYING HARD TO GET GETS OLD FAST. YOU'RE TRYING MY PATIENCE.
YOU'RE MAKING A MISTAKE!
LAST CHANCE.

HOLOFERNES, LISTEN TO ME!
OW! PLEASE- LET GO OF ME!
GET OUT.
...

GET AWAY FROM ME!
I WANT NOTHING TO DO WITH YOU!
I WISH I NEVER MET YOU!
STOP IT! GET OUT!
THIS IS ALL YOUR FAULT!
MY LORD?

LET ME HELP YOU—

IT'S BECAUSE OF YOU MY LIFE WILL NEVER GO BACK TO NORMAL!

NO! I DON'T NEED YOU!

SHUT UP! SHUT UP! SHUT UP! I'LL KILL YOU! I'LL KILL EVERYONE! THEN WHO WILL DEFY ME? NO ONE! NO ONE!

THUD
... NO ONE...
... DON'T
REJECT ME...

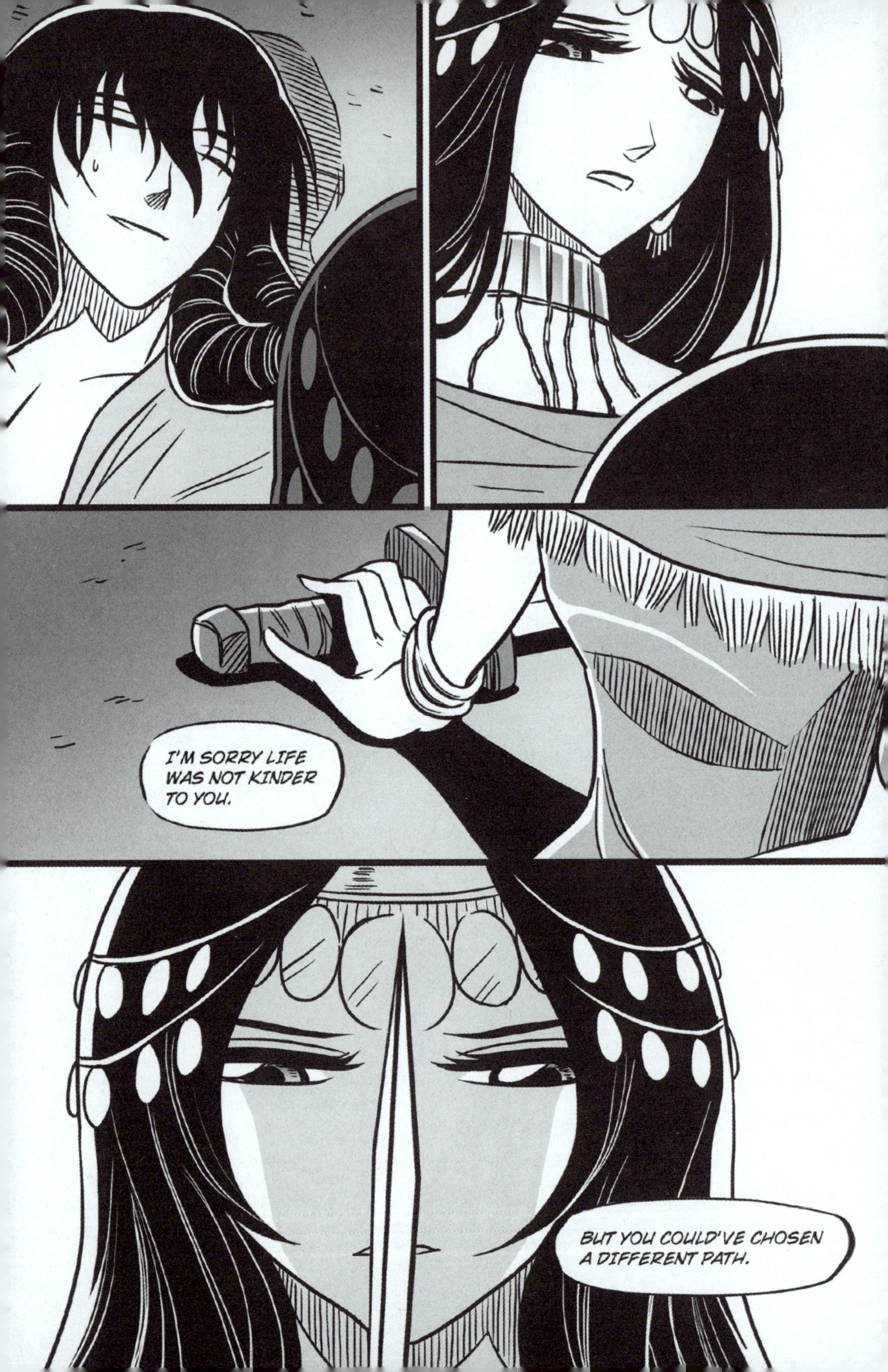

I'M SORRY LIFE WAS NOT KINDER TO YOU.
BUT YOU COULD'VE CHOSEN A DIFFERENT PATH.

GOD GIVE ME STRENGTH!

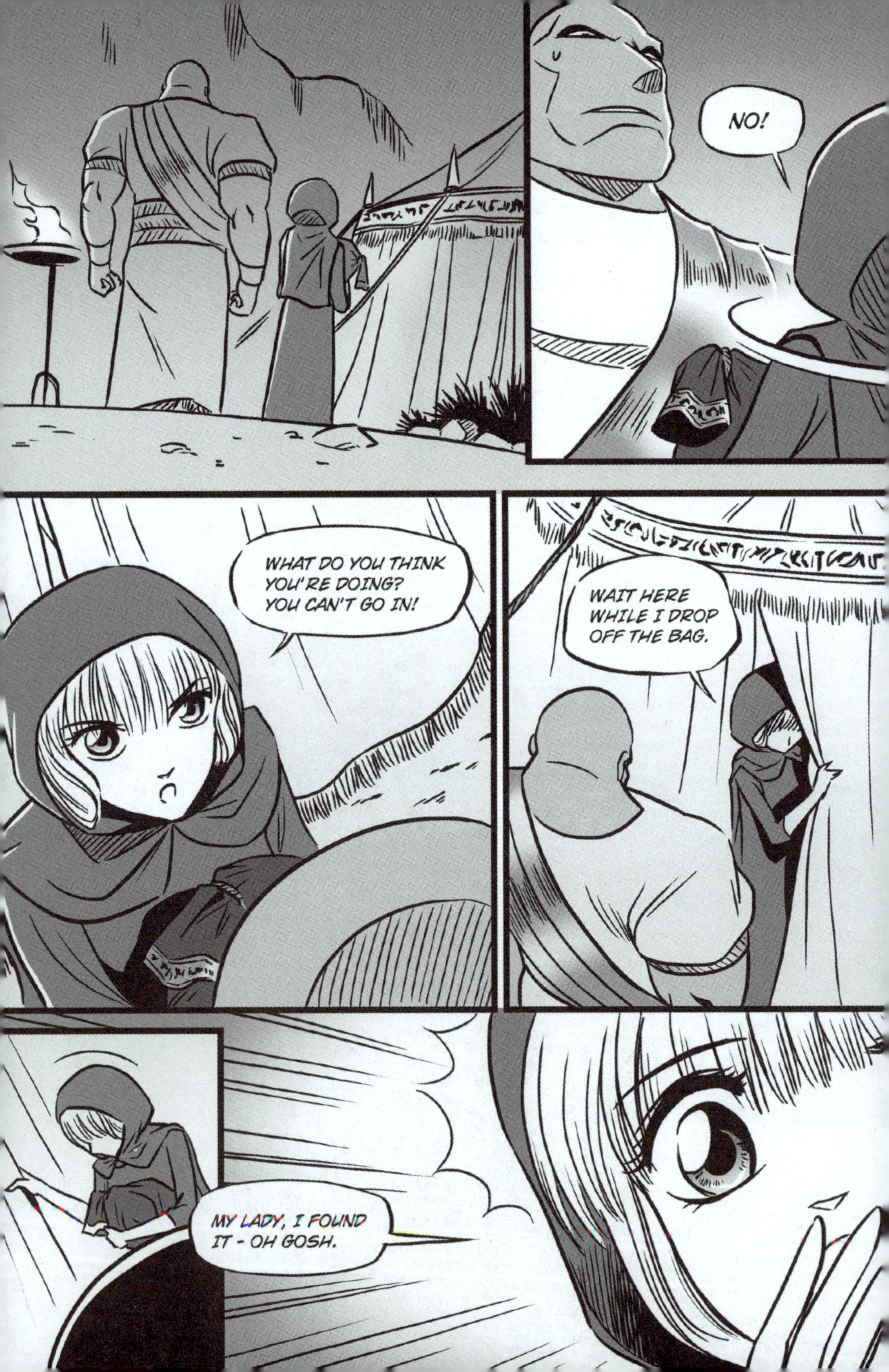

NO!
WHAT DO YOU THINK YOU'RE DOING? YOU CAN'T GO IN!
WAIT HERE WHILE I DROP OFF THE BAG.
MY LADY, I FOUND IT - OH GOSH.

JUDITH!
ARE YOU ALRIGHT?
YES, I'M FINE,...
I'M SORRY - I SHOULD'VE COME BACK SOONER.
YOU DID MARVELOUSLY. THANKS TO YOU I DIDN'T HAVE TO DRINK ANYTHING...
WHY DON'T YOU WAIT OUTSIDE. I'LL BE RIGHT OUT.

WELL?
OH! YES, THEY'RE DONE. SHE'LL BE COMING OUT IN A MOMENT.
YOUR MASTER IS QUITE EXHAUSTED — LET HIM SLEEP IT OFF.

COME ALONG ZUSA. IT'S TIME WE LEAVE.
THUD

MY LADY.

OPEN THE GATES!
... WE HAVE UNTIL THE END OF TODAY BY OUR OATH...
OPEN THE GATES!
PERHAPS WE SHOULD HOLD OFF OPENING THE GATES JUST A LITTLE LONGER!
THEY WOULD'VE BEEN HERE BY NOW...
JUST DO IT.

OPEN THE GA-
THEY'RE TOO LATE...
FIGURES APPROACHING!
HOW MANY ARE THERE?
HURRY AND OPEN THE GATES!
IT'S THE ASSYRIAN MESSENGERS!
OR THE SCOUTS!

TWO! ON FOOT —
IT CAN'T BE...
JUDITH! IT'S JUDITH AND HER HANDMAID!
OPEN THE GATES!
THERE IS NOTHING TO FEAR...

GOD IS STILL WITH US!
JUDITH! ZUSA!
ARE YOU ALL RIGHT? DID THEY DO ANYTHING TO YOU?
WE'RE SAFE.
THEY DID NOTHING.

ACHIOR!
THANK GOD...
ACHIOR...
I MUST ASK YOU TO CONFIRM HOLOFERNES' IDENTITY.

...EESH. THAT'S HIM ALRIGHT.
THANK THE LORD!
WE'RE SAVED!
IT'S NOT OVER YET...
DON'T GET TOO WORKED-UP. THERE'S STILL THE ENTIRE ASSYRIAN ARMY PARKED OUTSIDE.
ALL ABLE BODIED MEN, GATHER YOUR SPEARS AND SWORDS.

H-HEY! HEY, LOOK AT THIS!
THE ISRAELITES ARE ASSEMBLING!
NO WAY!
NOT GOOD—
SEND WORD TO THE LIEUTENANT!
HOW MUCH TROUBLE DO YOU THINK WE'D GET IN IF HE WAS... BUSY?
... WELL?... YOU GOING IN?...
I'M NOT GOING IN! YOU GO IN!
HOW MUCH TROUBLE DO YOU THINK YOU'D GET IN IF WE FAIL TO REPORT THIS?

WHAT'S THE PROBLEM?
SIR!
THE ISRAELITES ARE LINING UP FOR BATTLE SIR!
AND WE WOULD TELL HOLOFERNES BUT... WE DON'T KNOW IF HE'S... PREOCCUPIED.
THE WOMAN AND HER HANDMAID LEFT FOR PRAYER AFTER MIDNIGHT LAST NIGHT, AS ALWAYS.
YOU SURE?
COWARDS.

MY LORD?
WHAT...?
MY LORD??
FLOP

HE IS AWAKENING NOW-
WHERE IS LORD HOLOFERNES? WE HAVEN'T A MOMENT TO LOSE!
WAKE HIM UP IMMEDIATELY!
I WONDER WHAT THE FIGHTING WILL BE LIKE...
HOLOFERNES WILL KNOW HOW TO BEAT THEM.
WHAT ARE HIS ORDERS, BAGOAS?
KLANK
HOLY-

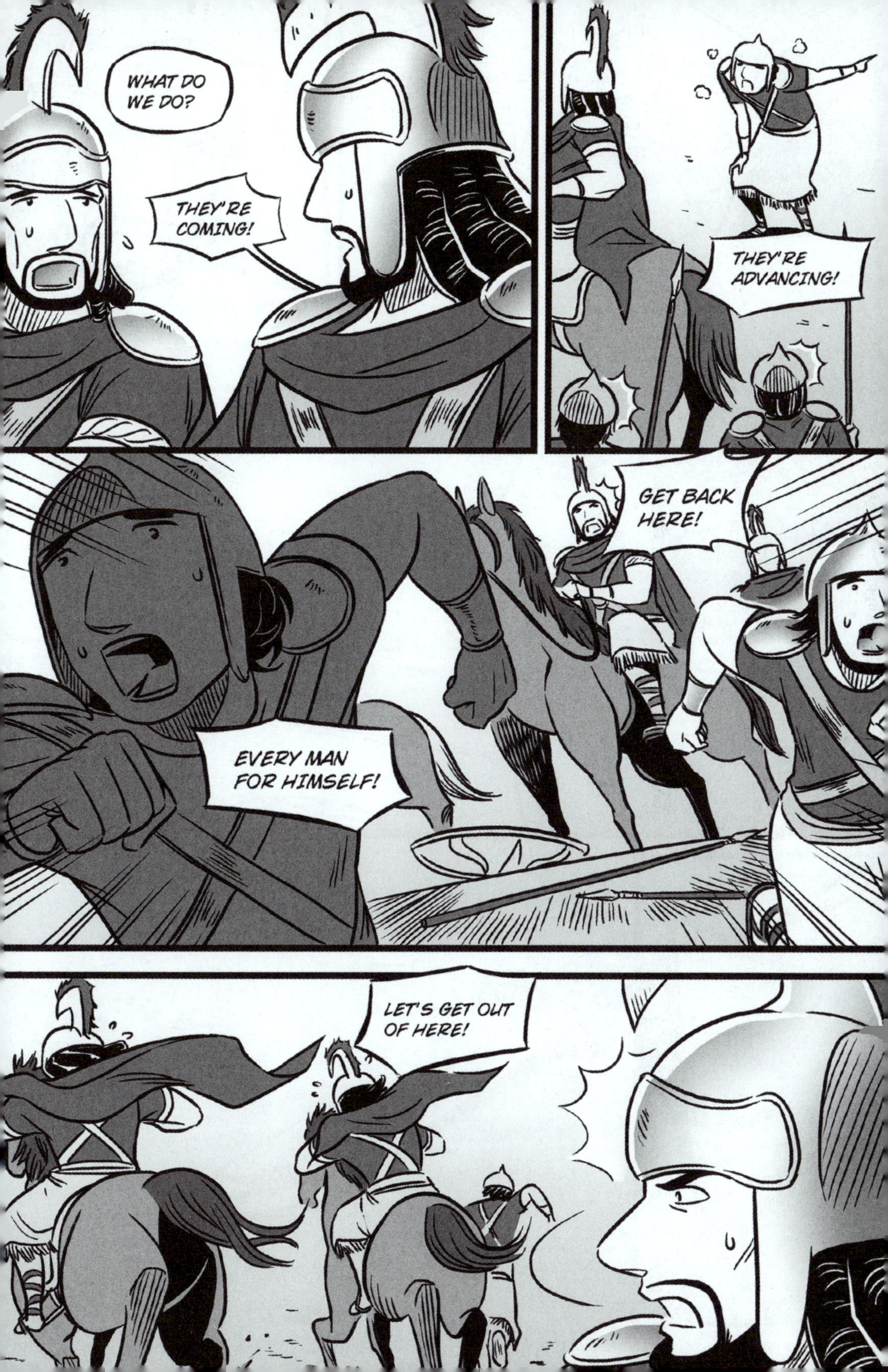

WHAT DO WE DO?
THEY'RE COMING!
THEY'RE ADVANCING!
GET BACK HERE!
EVERY MAN FOR HIMSELF!
LET'S GET OUT OF HERE!

COWARDS! DESERTERS!
IT'S OVER...

"FEAR AND TREMBLING CAME OVER THEM, SO THAT THEY DID NOT WAIT FOR ONE ANOTHER,
... BUT WITH ONE IMPULSE ALL RUSHED OUT
AND FLED BY EVERY PATH ACROSS THE PLAIN AND THROUGH THE HILL COUNTRY" JUDITH 15:2
"THEN THE MEN OF ISRAEL, EVERY ONE THAT WAS A SOLDIER...
WITH ONE ACCORD THEY FELL UPON THE ENEMY AND CUT THEM DOWN." JUDITH 15:3-5

"SO ALL THE PEOPLE PLUNDERED THE CAMP...
THEY GAVE JUDITH THE TENT OF HOLOFERNES AND ALL HIS SILVER..." JUDITH 15:11

YOU ARE BLESSED BY THE MOST HIGH GOD ABOVE ALL WOMEN ON EARTH... BECAUSE IN WALKING THE STRAIGHT PATH BEFORE OUR GOD YOU DID NOT SPARE YOUR OWN LIFE.
YOU ARE THE EXALTATION OF JERUSALEM... AND GOD IS WELL PLEASED WITH IT.

"AND SHE WENT BEFORE ALL THE PEOPLE IN THE DANCE, LEADING ALL THE WOMEN, WHILE ALL THE MEN OF ISRAEL FOLLOWED, BEARING THEIR ARMS AND WEARING GARLANDS AND WITH SONGS ON THEIR LIPS."
JUDITH 15:13
"AND WHEN ACHIOR SAW ALL THAT THE GOD OF ISRAEL HAD DONE... HE WAS CIRCUMCISED AND AND JOINED THE HOUSE OF ISRAEL..." JUDITH 14:10
"THANK YOU... FOR NEVER LEAVING MY SIDE..."

KNOCK
KNOCK

OH! HEY, JUDITH.

HELLO ACHIOR. DOES THIS MEAN YOU'RE LEAVING US?

WHAT? OH. YEAH. I'LL BE HEADING OUT PRESENTLY. IT'S ABOUT TIME I GOT BACK TO MY PEOPLE – THAT IS, IF THEY'LL HAVE ME BACK... BUT I THOUGHT I'D STOP TO SAY GOODBYE.

I'M SORRY TO HEAR THAT. WE WILL CERTAINLY MISS YOU. AND YOU WILL ALWAYS BE WELCOME HERE IF EVER YOU DECIDE TO RETURN.

THANKS. HEY, LISTEN...

BEFORE I LEAVE... WELL... I'M ALSO HERE TO TAKE CARE OF SOME LAST MINUTE BUSINESS.
HMM?
YEAH, UM – YOU SEE, JUDITH, HERE'S THE THING, I WANTED TO ASK YOU SOMETHING...
I'D HOPE I WOULDN'T HAVE TO DO THIS TO YOU TOO. LET ME BE FRANK.
SIGH
I'M SORRY ACHIOR, BUT NO. I'M FLATTERED, BUT FOR THE LAST TIME, I'M NOT ACCEPTING ANYONE'S HAND.
AND IF I GET ONE MORE MAN ON MY DOORSTEP...

... EH... NO, NO, YOU'RE MISTAKEN...
... HUH?...
I'M NOT AFTER YOUR HAND...
HA HA HA
OH I SEE... PLEASE, COME IN.
ARE YOU SURE?
YES...

SHE'S OUT BACK.
I GOT YOUR LETTER.
OH! ACHIOR-
SPLISH
OH GOSH- I AM SO SORRY!
DON'T WORRY ABOUT IT -

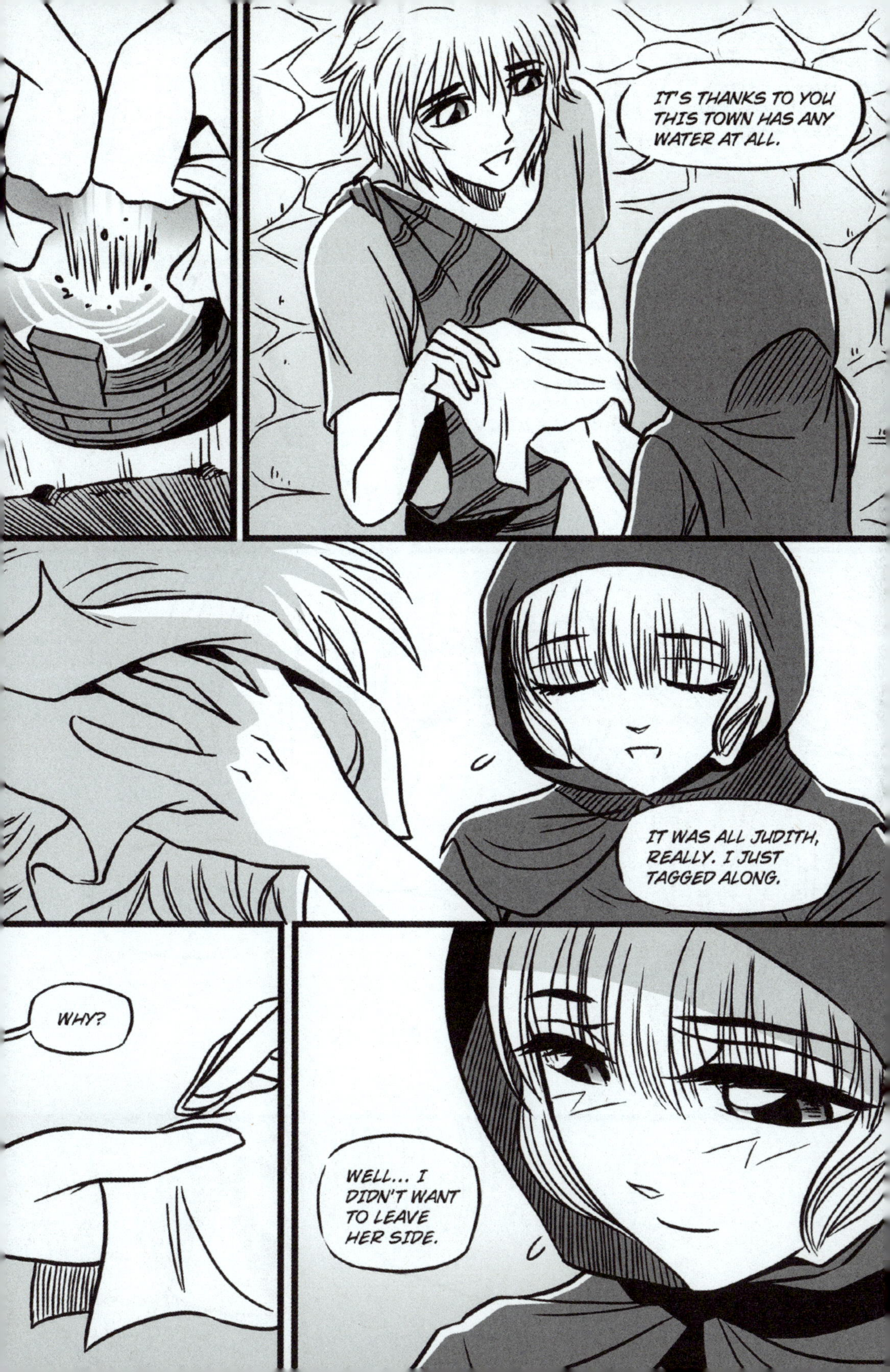
IT'S THANKS TO YOU THIS TOWN HAS ANY WATER AT ALL.
IT WAS ALL JUDITH, REALLY. I JUST TAGGED ALONG.
WHY?
WELL... I DIDN'T WANT TO LEAVE HER SIDE.

THAT'S PRETTY RECKLESS, DON'T YOU THINK?
I MEAN... SPONTANEOUSLY LEAVING EVERYTHING BEHIND JUST TO BE WITH SOMEONE YOU LOVE?
YEAH, IT WAS PRETTY RECKLESS, WASN'T IT?
YOU UP FOR DOING IT AGAIN?
...HUH?

JUDITH! JUDITH! YOU'LL NEVER BELIEVE IT! ACHIOR ASKED ME TO MARRY HIM! HE DIDN'T EVEN ASK FOR A DOWRY!
I'M SO HAPPY FOR YOU, ZUSA. HE REALLY LOVES YOU.
BUT I HAD TO REFUSE.
WHAT? WHY WOULD YOU DO THAT?
I WORK FOR YOU, JUDITH. I MAY NOT NEED A DOWRY, BUT I STILL HAVE ANOTHER 5 YEARS OF SERVICE BEFORE MY MOTHER'S DEBT IS PAID.

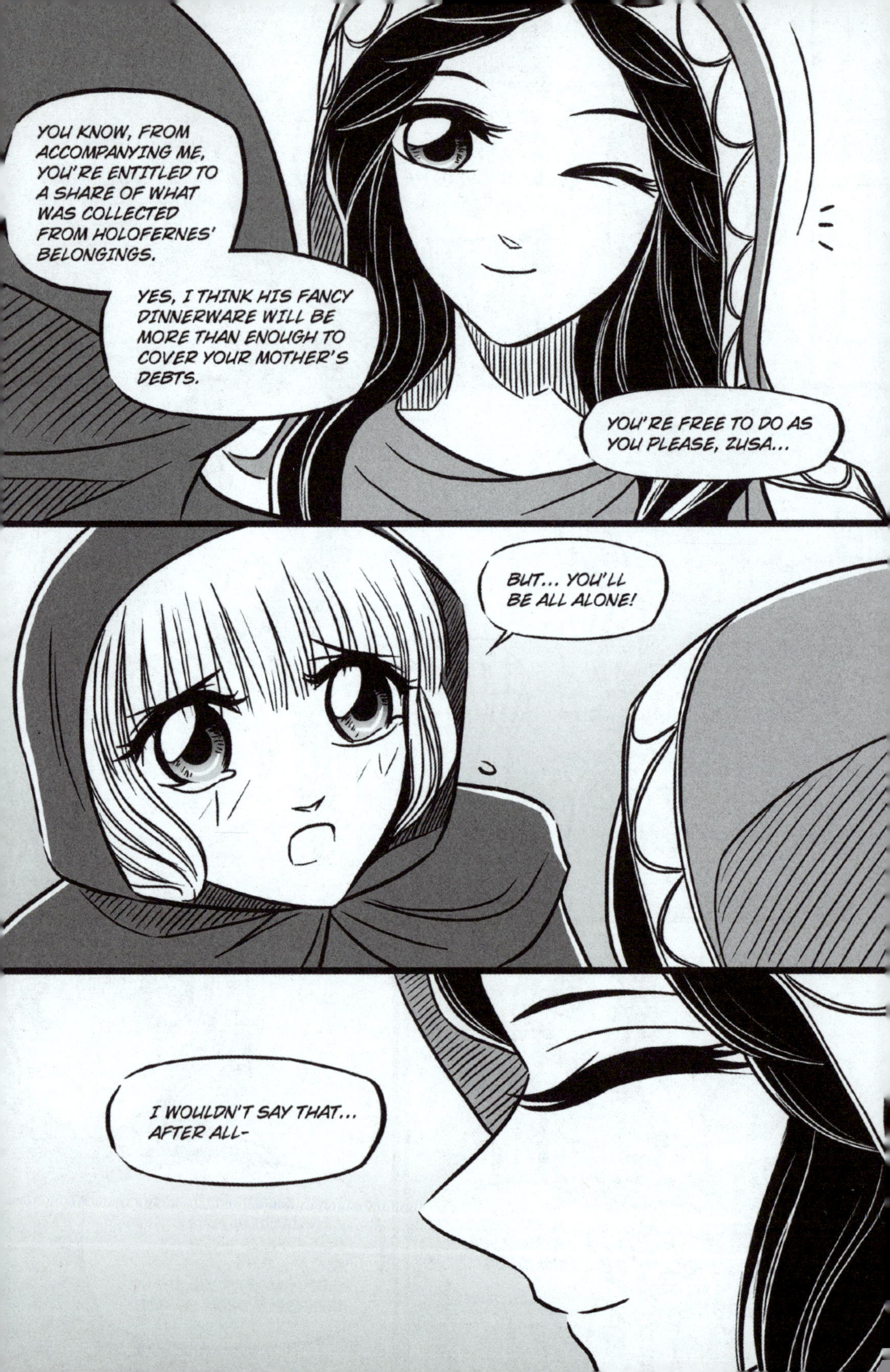

YOU KNOW, FROM ACCOMPANYING ME, YOU'RE ENTITLED TO A SHARE OF WHAT WAS COLLECTED FROM HOLOFERNES' BELONGINGS.
YES, I THINK HIS FANCY DINNERWARE WILL BE MORE THAN ENOUGH TO COVER YOUR MOTHER'S DEBTS.
YOU'RE FREE TO DO AS YOU PLEASE, ZUSA...
BUT... YOU'LL BE ALL ALONE!
I WOULDN'T SAY THAT... AFTER ALL—

WHEN YOU LOVE SOMEONE, THEY NEVER REALLY LEAVE YOU.
YOU WILL ALWAYS BE MY BEST AND TRUEST FRIEND, ZUSA.

"AND NO ONE EVER AGAIN SPREAD TERROR AMONG THE PEOPLE OF ISRAEL..."
"IN THE DAYS OF JUDITH..."

"OR FOR A LONG TIME AFTER HER DEATH."
JUDITH 16:25
fin.

Judith's Prayer

Judith is recognized as one of the Bible's heroines. She demonstrated a great trust in God to save her and her people. Her story can still inspire us today to trust God and remain faithful in prayer. Here is part of her prayer to God, found in the Old Testament Book of Judith:

"For your strength does not depend on numbers, nor your might on the powerful. But you are the God of the lowly, helper of the oppressed, upholder of the weak, protector of the forsaken, savior of those without hope. Please, please, God of my father, God of the heritage of Israel, Lord of heaven and earth, Creator of the waters, King of all your creation, hear my prayer!"

-Judith 9:11–12